Bedtime Meditation Relaxation Stories for kids

A collection of positive meditation stories to help babies and toddlers fall asleep fast in bed and have a relaxing night's sleep filled with colorful beautiful dreams

Sofia Fairy Woods

© Copyright 2021 - All rights reserved.

The content of this book cannot be reproduced, duplicated or transmitted without the direct written permission of the author or publisher.

Under no circumstances will you be guilty or legally responsible

against the publisher, or the author, for any damages, reparations,

or monetary loss due to the information contained in this book either directly or indirectly.

Legal warning:

This book is protected by copyright. This book is for personal use only.

You may not modify, distribute, sell, use, quote or paraphrase

part, or the content of this book, without the consent of the author or editor.

Disclaimer Notice:

Please note that the information contained in this document is for educational and entertainment purposes only. All the effort has been executed to present accurate, up-to-date and reliable information, complete information. No warranties of any kind are made or implied. Readers acknowledge that the author does not participate in the provision of legal, financial, medical or professional advice. The content of this book has been derived from various sources. Consult a licensed professional before attempting any techniques described in this book. By reading this document, the reader accepts that under no circumstances is the author responsible for any loss, direct or indirect, incurred as a result of the use of information contained in this document, including, but not limited to, the following: errors, omissions or inaccuracies.

Table of Contents

TALES AND STORIES FOR CHILDREN WHO HAVE A TANTRUM 1

ISAAC'S ROOM AND HIS DOLLS, THROWING TANTRUMS. 3

THE KITCHEN HE DIDN'T WANT TO COOK. 8

WHY PLAY THE KITCHEN GAME. 13

THE CAT OF PIZZA. 15

LITTLE CHILDREN CHEF 19

RECIPE FOR CHILDREN: THE CAT OF PIZZA 27

RECIPE WITH HIPPO AND TOY KITCHEN. 29

COOKING GAMES: NOAH, MOM AND THE HIPPO. 30

RECIPE FOR CHILDREN: BAKED HIPPO. 34

PLAY KITCHEN - JACOB, CAMILA AND THE SNOWMAN. 36

JACOB, CAMILA AND THE SNOWMAN. .. 39

RECIPE FOR CHILDREN: CHRISTMAS SNOWMAN. 46

HISTORY OF WOODEN LETTERS. 48

STORY TO READ TO CHILDREN: STORY OF WOODEN LETTERS AND MAGIC WORDS. 50

MARTA AND SANTA'S COOKIES. 55

RECIPE FOR CHILDREN: SANTA CLAUS COOKIES. 68

WHY PLAY BY COPYING THE GREATS? 71

SANTA'S COOKIES - MARTHA AND THE CHRISTMAS STARS.. 74

STORIES AND MAGIC: READING FOR CHILDREN. 79

HISTORY OF CANDY TO GROW UP.......... 81

CHILDREN'S READINGS AND ROAD SIGNS... 86

READING FOR CHILDREN: PETER, THE UNKNOWN CITY AND THE GAME OF TRAFFIC SIGNS. 88

WHEN CHILDREN HAVE A TANTRUM 94

LEO'S SWORD WHEN HE THROWS TOO MANY TANTRUMS. 96

FAIRY TALES FOR CHILDREN: THE CHOCOLATE OF CALM. 100

CHILDREN'S FEARS: A TALE TO SOOTHE CHILDREN. 107

THE MARABESÙ CRYING IN THE WOODS. 109

WHEN CHILDREN HAVE A TANTRUM .. 116

THE LITTLE MONKEY WHO ALWAYS WANTED TO STAY AWAKE 118

TALES FOR CHILDREN TO GROW UP TOGETHER. 125

LACKY FOX CUB WHO DID NOT LISTEN. 127

STORIES FOR CHILDREN; GROWING TOGETHER WITH THE RULES 131

THE SCHOOL WITHOUT RULES AND THE SCHOOL WITH TOO MANY RULES 133

HISTORY AND MAGIC. 140

HISTORY AND MAGIC: THE MAGIC OF THE GOLDFISH. 141

CHILDREN'S STORIES TO READ ABOUT NAUGHTY CHILDREN................................. 147

FABLE ABOUT THE WHIMS OF CHILDREN; ALADDIN CHILD BRAT....... 149

LEGENDS AND POPULAR STORIES. 154

MARTIN AND THE BIG BEAR. 156

THE METAPHOR OF THE RAINBOW. 162

HOW THE RAINBOW WAS FORMED. 164

CHILDREN'S FAIRY TALES AND LEGENDS... 170

THE GAME BENCH....................................... 172

CHILDREN'S TALES ABOUT LACING. ... 177

THE STRANGE LAND OF LACING........... 179

WELCOME TO THE COUNTRY OF LACES 182

DIDACTIC FABLE FOR CHILDREN. 186

ELI, THE DIDACTIC CLOCK. 187

FABLE ABOUT CHILDREN'S FEARS. 193

THE PUPPY WHO WAS AFRAID OF THE DARK. 194

CHILDREN'S STORY TO READ BEFORE GOING TO SLEEP 200

EDWIN WAS A CHILD WHO DID NOT WANT TO GO TO SLEEP. 202

CHILDREN'S FAIRY TALES ABOUT WHIMS. 206

SAM THE CHAMELEON AND THE WHIMS OF THE MORNING. 208

NORA AND THE SECRET INGREDIENT. 213

RECIPE FOR CHILDREN: SOFT CAKE AT COCOA 223

SOFT COCOA CAKE - NORA IS THE SECRET INGREDIENT 225

Tales and stories for children who have a tantrum.

Dear mothers, this fairytale tells about the room of the dolls that have tantrums; this fairytale is very special.

It is a "refuge of emotions," a place where children can express what they feel, calm down when they get angry, untie the difficult knots of tantrums, be comforted if they are sad, reassured if they are afraid.

The room of the whimsical dolls, this story for children, is magical. But we hope that there is something similar in reality; a way to recognize feelings, accept them, overcome them when they put us in difficulty.

Isaac's room and his dolls, throwing tantrums.

Isaac has a doll room in his room. It is a real wooden bedroom, with furniture, chairs, tables, a doll's stroller and a cradle. He is a very free and peaceful child because his parents have always made him play with what he preferred. Isaac has two dolls: one of the two is always good, and the other is a little naughty. The two dolls sometimes quarrel, the naughty doll bullies. It doesn't follow the rules and doesn't listen to the good doll.

When Isaac gets angry, the naughty doll is even more disobedient. Monday comes, and Isaac is angry with everyone. In the morning, Isaac doesn't want to go to kindergarten. In the afternoon, he doesn't want to go home. Isaac is angry with the teachers, his mother, his kindergarten friends, and his little sister. When the mother goes to pick up Isaac from kindergarten, the child doesn't want to go home. His mom dresses him and takes him out, and Isaac throws a tantrum on the street; he cries and screams and doesn't want to walk. By the time they get home, his mom has already lost her temper.

"Go to the bedroom and try to calm down on your own," his mom says and leaves him alone.

Isaac enters the doll room. His little friends start arguing, and the disobedient doll tells the child:

"Today, we are even angrier!"

"Yes, today I want to throw everything up in the air!" Isaac replies, red in the face.

"Let's do it!" Says the doll. Isaac has a box of toys; he takes them all out and throws them into the floor. They bring out the colors from the packaging, the wooden puzzle pieces, the paints to paint and all the plastic constructions. In the bedroom, now, there is a lot of confusion, but Isaac and the doll are even angrier. The good doll exclaims, "Enough! Calm down, you two, or mom will come, and she'll be really mad!". The naughty doll replies: "I don't care. I want to throw everything up in the air!" "Isaac," mum yells from the kitchen, "what is this noise?" Mom's voice is calm but curious. Isaac knows that she will soon be in the room, and then she will be really annoyed by all the toys scattered on the floor. "Dolls," Isaac says, "Make peace now." "We don't want to make peace," the bratty doll shouts. Too late, Mom came to the room.

"Mom," says Isaac, "the two dolls had a fight. The naughty doll just doesn't want to listen." Mom makes a weird face; after a second, she takes a breath and says, "Shall we tidy up together? Little by little, one by one," Mom puts away a toy; after she, is Isaac's turn, and she puts away another toy, little by little. The two dolls make peace.

The kitchen he didn't want to cook.

Dear ladies and gentlemen, kind mum and dad of the two little witches… er… er… adorable little girls who play with me every day, I introduce myself, although you already know me very well, I am Lina, the wooden toy kitchen.

I have lived in this house for a very long time, three years, since you took me from the shop where I was born and, as a prisoner, you took me to this noisy and colorful place that you call home.

At first, I was happy to play with little Savannah; she was tender, soft and plump. Her three-year-old little hands stroked me happily, and I spent my days baking imaginary cookies. I also cooked mountains of pasta with Nutella and wool balls for the meat sauce, but I was happy.

After a year of intense activity, a kind of Attila in a skirt arrives in our restaurant. On the first play, he took a knob apart; on the second, he hammered me with the head of his favorite doll, and she was only one year old! As the months went by, Attila - the one you call Dakota - began to involve the tender Savannah in his wild games of her. Other than biscuits and cakes, the Circus began here.

Not being able to completely disassemble myself, Attila invented a new pastime: climbing on drawers. How he climbed, I don't know; he was so fast and agile. I just know that it had become impossible to cook even a simple jam crepe with Savannah. Now, things have gotten so bad that I really can't take it anymore. So, from today, I stop cooking. Strike! Strike! Strike!

And it is useless for you to try to convince me: I will never cook with those two again, because before it was only Dakota, now it is still **Contribuirhe** Savannah, the tender, sweet and chubby Savannah, trying to pull the doors off me. Don't tell me she won't make it, because I already know it myself! However, I do not find it right that you play with my splendid figure like this.

I am a wooden kitchen; I am a classy kitchen, me!

So, ladies and gentlemen, kind mum and dad of the two harpies ... er ... little girls, dear fathers and mothers of the little pests ... er ... darlings, from today, I cross the stove, barricade the sink, raise barricades between my worktops and the rest of the room.

I'll go back to cooking, just and only in case, calm the two demons ... Er ... girls, harmony returns to this kitchen, resume drinking imaginary coffee with the grandmothers and preparing ham sandwiches for snacks.

Otherwise, remember, I turn my heels and walk away with a high hood.

Dear Children, We apologize for the inconvenience,

but - for today - it will not be possible to drink imaginary coffee or prepare fabulous recipes.

RISTO-CHILD

will remain closed for Strike!

The staff

Why play the kitchen game.

The cooking game is a very useful and instructive entertainment for children aged two and over. Our little ones, in fact, already naturally carry out constant learning through playful activity and the imitation of adult gestures, and they also have a lot of fun preparing the most imaginative and greedy recipes.

In all respects, the play kitchen involves them even more in the game, helping them develop logical thinking, psychomotor skills, the emotional sphere, and socialization. In particular, this story aims to offer children some useful notions on food and provide a starting point for parents and teachers, since nothing makes children happier than, for example, kneading.

Kneading and putting their hands in different materials is a great exercise for their manual and sensory skills, and with an adult by their side to learn and have fun with, they will feel safe and appreciated.

The Cat of pizza.

"Good morning, children!" she greeted them, smiling that morning. "Today we will learn to eat well and prepare something good; then we move to our corner of the ..." "... kitchen!" the children exclaimed.

They always had a lot of fun preparing the most whimsical dishes dictated by their imagination in the large play kitchen of the school, modular and identical to that of the adults but made to measure children and all of the scented wood.

"Good little ones! Now, first of all, let's put on all the aprons and the chef's hats," said the teacher. "Mattew, Francesco, Mia, and Giuly, here is one each; I'll help you."

Once the little cooks were dressed, the teacher began to explain to them:

"If we want to cook well, we must also know how to eat well. Eating right is very important because it makes us grow well, gives us the energy to do many things and keeps diseases away. Now let's play a game to recognize flavors."

She took four bottles containing liquids and continued, "Our tongue recognizes four different types of flavors; do you know what they are?" "Nooo," the little ones answered in chorus.

"They are the sweet, salty, bitter and sour flavors," the teacher continued to explain "let's see if you can recognize them," and she poured the liquid from one of the bottles, which was made up of water and sugar into some glasses.

"Taste it and tell me: is it sweet, salty, bitter or sour?" "Sweet," Mia replied.

"Very good! And this other one, what does it taste like? " and she poured them water with salt. "Salty," Mattew said.

"Bravo, Mattew! And this one more? " this time, she poured them some sugar-free decaffeinated coffee. "Amaroooo" shouted Francesco.

"Bravo you too, Francesco. And the latest flavor?" and she poured them water with lemon. "Acid," Giuly said with a grimace. "Brava Giuly!" said the teacher. "Now what about cooking me something? You are free to use all the materials that are here." "Yeeeeeeeeeeeeeeeeeeeeeeeeeeeeeee," the children exclaimed, getting into the play kitchen.

Little children chef.

After a while, the teacher came up and asked, "What have you prepared, Mia?"
"A fried egg, teacher!" replied the child.
"With some cotton and a red ball, dude!" the teacher appreciated "and you, Mattew?"
"I made pasta with tomato," said the boy. It was made up of red plastic bricks and yellow pegs, all of the same material, plastic. "Mmm,

it looks good!" The teacher smiled. "And you two who are cooking?" she asked Giuly and Francesco.

"Cutlets with vegetables," replied the children as they flattened the clay with their plump little hands to complete their dish.

"Very well, children," the teacher said, satisfied. "Do you know that you have prepared some very important dishes for our body?

Eggs and cutlets, in fact, contain the proteins that make us grow, pasta contains carbohydrates that give us the energy to do many things and vegetables contain vitamins that protect us from disease. That do you think we transform them into real food?"

"Yes, come on, teacher! Make us a spell." the children screamed.

The teacher then took a turn on herself. His long red hair and her dress sparkled, then she said three magic words and - poof! - foods made of cotton, plastic and plasticine were transformed into fried eggs, pasta and tomatoes, cutlets with real vegetables and the classroom was filled with their good scent. "Wooow!" the children exclaimed in wonder. They knew their teacher was actually a fairy, but they always gasped when she did her magic.

"Today is Mattew's birthday. How about if, as a gift, we prepare his favorite food? What do you like best, Mattew?" suggested the teacher-fairy. "Mmm," she thought about the child, "The pizza!"

"Very well!" exclaimed the teacher amid the enthusiasm of the children, always happy when it came to kneading. "To make a good pizza, we need flour, yeast, water, salt and oil. To dress it, you need tomatoes, mozzarella, oregano, and other ingredients of our choice, "and with a gesture, she magically made everything necessary appear.

Thus, she taught them to arrange the flour "in a fountain," in the center, they added the yeast and lukewarm water, and with great fun, they knead everything well, adding salt and oil. "Perfect kids! Now, we cover the dough with a cloth and let it rise in a warm place. What does it mean to make the dough rise, you know?

"Nooo," said Francesco.

"It means having patience and waiting for about an hour and a half because the yeast needs this time to make the dough swell and soft, so when we eat it, it will be tastier," said the teacher. "But an hour and a half is a long time!" Francesco pouted impatiently. "Okay, this time, I'll do magic to make it rise right away. In the meantime, we will mash the tomatoes and season them with oil and salt, then we will slice the mozzarella," the teacher smiled, and so they did.

Then they spread the pasta on a baking sheet greased with oil and poured the tomato they had crushed over it. "Now, the dough should be left to rise for another hour, but I'll do another magic so it will be ready immediately, okay Francesco?" laughed the teacher. "Yup!" the child exclaims, laughing too.

The fairy spoke some magic words, and immediately, the dough leavened at the right point, then she said other words making a gesture towards the oven of the play kitchen and, magically, it lit up and began to heat up. "When the oven or kitchen stove is on, you have to be very careful not to touch them. Never even touch hot pots and pans, or you could burn yourself and get very hurt," the teacher warned them, putting the pan in the oven, and continued, "Every food put to cook in the oven needs the right temperature and the right cooking time.

The pizza should be cooked in a preheated oven at 220°ᶜ for about 20 minutes."

Play to cook pizza.

In short, the pizza was ready. The teacher-fairy took it out of the oven, and while the exquisite perfume made everyone's mouth water, she announced, "Mmm, that's good! Now I will teach you to do another magic: to turn pizza into a cat." "A cattttttttttt?" Mia asked in amazement, "And how is it done?" "It's easy," said the teacher, cutting the pizza still in the pan into six smaller squares. "See? We now have these six pizzas. We put two round slices of mozzarella on top and, on top of each mozzarella slice, we put half an olive to make the eyes; we will use two mushrooms to make the ears; for the nose, we will use a small slice of salami, for the mustache, we will use six sausage sticks, three to the right and three to the left of the salami nose and half a slice of tomato for the mouth. We put a little oregano on top, and our very nice pizza cat is ready!" the teacher laughed at seeing all the children with their mouths open in surprise.

"Have you seen? Everyone can do magic; just use a little imagination!"

Even the children laughed happily. They had learned so many things that day at school. They baked the pan for another 5 minutes, just long enough to melt the mozzarella, added a little more oil as a final touch and, at that point, they did one last magic: in a few minutes, they made all the pizzas disappear!

Recipe for children:
The Cat of pizza

ဝင်ဘာနိုင်ငံနိုင်ငံသားများ

If you want to make the pizza that was described in this story, you need these ingredients:

500g of flour, 250ml of water, 500g of peeled tomatoes, 20g of oil, 15g of yeast, 10g of salt,

2 mozzarella, 2 tablespoons of extra virgin olive oil oregano.

Other condiments to taste: olives, a tomato, some frankfurters, small slices of salami, champignon mushrooms and whatever you like!

Recipe with hippo and toy kitchen.

Dear parents, they say that having young children makes children again, as does Noah's mother, who tells her son about when she and hero holder brother played with the wooden toy kitchen, found as a gift for a fabulous Christmas… The story told here can stimulate children to exercise the sense of memory.

Cooking games: Noah, mom and the hippo.

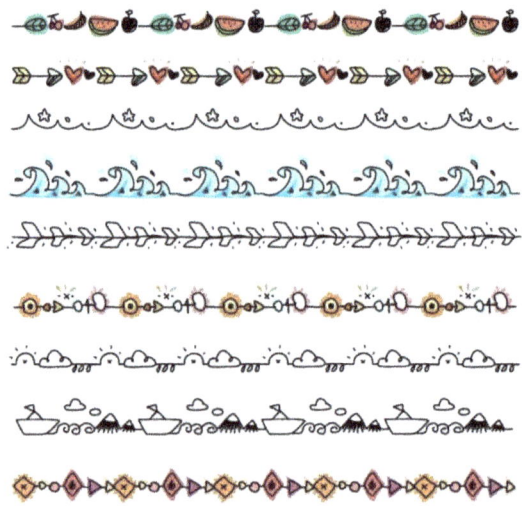

"Mom, tell me a story," asked little six-year-old Noah,

"Of course, my love," replied the mother, and she began, "I'll tell you about the time when Uncle Liam and I were little and, for Christmas, we found a fantastic wooden toy kitchen under the tree, a gift from Grandma

Anna. I was four years old, and my uncle five years old. Grandma gave us a great gift, as long as we both used it together, without ever arguing. When we opened the huge package, I was speechless; I still remember it. On the other hand, Uncle Liam began to jump for joy throughout the dining room; it was a great joy for him, who always remained enchanted to watch his mother cook. The days went by, and we always played with the toy kitchen, inventing many stories and many recipes, like the time we cooked a hippo. "

"A hippo? I do not believe it!" chuckled Noah, already a great expert on animals. "Don't tell lies!"

"No, no, what a lie… All true! Listen, I'll tell you how. You take a hippo that's not too big, don't you believe me? You take it to the river because they don't sell it in the supermarket. Then it is placed in a giant pan and seasoned with sauce and parsley. The recipe was just like that, trust and listen. Then you take a plate from the kitchen cabinet and pour the oil. Then…"

"Mom, what are you saying? This recipe doesn't exist!"

"You are right. Let's put the hippo away. But we really cooked pasta with meat sauce, you know? Get a big pasta pot; Uncle Liam used to say. And I took it. And then take a small pot for the sauce, he added. And I did that too. And while we waited for the sauce and pasta to be ready, we sat down to drink coffee, as you do now with your doll friends."

"But it's a fake coffee."

"You say? It looks very good to me. If you close your eyes, you seem to smell, like when you were four, and you cooked my steak with your toy kitchen. Do you remember?"
"Siiiiiiiiii! But now I'm grown up, I really cook." "So, are we going to give the children's kitchen to someone younger, honey?"
"No... Maybe one day, we'll cook a hippo together."

Recipe for children: baked hippo.

If you want to make the hippo recipe, you need these ingredients:

One hippopotamus is not too big; one can of peeled tomatoes, parsley salt and pepper to taste extra virgin olive oil, a pan of adequate size, a large oven.

When cooked, don't forget to decorate the hippopotamus with a sprinkling of chopped fresh parsley and lemon slices.

Mom, what are you saying? There is no such recipe!

Play Kitchen - Jacob, Camila and the Snowman.

Why play the toy kitchen game?
The toy kitchen game is an imitative game involving children aged two and over capable of combining useful with pleasure, boys and girls freely. The little ones, in fact, not only constantly learn through play and imitation of

the gestures of adults, which are a point of reference for them, but also have a lot of fun preparing the most imaginative recipes with their toy kitchen, which being in all and for all similar to that of the greats, including accessories, it offers an even more exciting gaming experience. It is a very instructive and useful entertainment to develop their imagination and creativity and everything that has to do with logical thinking, emotions, psychomotor skills, and socialization.

If you add to all this even a minimum of teaching by adults, the toy kitchen can become a real growth laboratory, thanks to which the child will be able to form a wealth of notions that will be useful in future life.

Just like in this story, in which the two children protagonists, with their grandmother's help, make an easy and delicious Christmas recipe and learn that with a little imagination, even the lack of snow can be overcome.

Jacob, Camila and the snowman.

It was the morning of Christmas Eve, and two little brothers, Jacob and Camila, were watching TV with their grandmother. They were a bit bored because it was cold and raining heavily for several days and they had not been able to go out.

It would have been nice to go for a walk with mum and dad to enjoy the festive air among the illuminated shop windows and, above all, to go under the big Christmas tree in the main square of the city, full of intermittent colored lights, but anything! Of too much rain we had to stay at home.

Fortunately, their favorite cartoon was on the air shortly after, and the children started to watch it very amused. In that episode, the protagonist, a child named Jo, was struggling to con the snow. One night it snowed on his village, and the next morning, when he woke up, it was all white: the streets, the roofs, the park and Jo and the other children who lived there, delighted, ran out to play with snowballs.

At one point, they also made a giant snowman starting from three large piles of snow that they worked with their hands to obtain three large balls: a larger one for the legs, a little smaller for the body and an even smaller one for the head. Then with bits of coal, they made eyes and teeth; with a carrot, they made the nose, with small stones the buttons of the jacket and with two dry branches the arms. Finally, they put a nice hat on his head and a long scarf around his neck. "Look, grandma, how beautiful the snowman is!" Jacob exclaimed. "Yes, it's really nice," said the grandmother.

"Grandma, but here with us when it snows?" Camila asked. "Oh, my darling," answered the grandmother, "unfortunately, it doesn't snow often here. The last time was a long time ago."

"Ugh," the little girl pouted, "but then we can never do the snowman!" "Why not? We can't do it with snow, but a snowman if you want, we can do it anyway," said the grandmother smiling.

"Yesssssssss let's do it!" the two children screamed in chorus. "How about if we prepare a puppet that can also be eaten?" proposed the grandmother. "So tomorrow for Christmas lunch, we will make a nice surprise to mom and dad and uncles!" "Yesssss come on!" the children approved. "Okay," said the grandmother, "then we will make a delicious cheese puppet!". "A cheese puppet?" Jacob repeated in amazement.

"Yes, of cheese!" answered the grandmother. "I'll teach you how to do it, so next time you can do it yourself." "Can we do it with my toy kitchen?" Camila asked, opening her eyes wide. She loved her wooden kitchen, she was her favorite toy, and she spent hours and hours preparing exquisite dishes for her dolls and friends.

"Sure!" the grandmother answered. "I'm going to get everything we need. In the meantime, wash your hands and sit in the chairs of your table next to the play kitchen," and she left the room. The children obeyed, and shortly after, the grandmother, entering their room, found them already seated and ready to start.

"Well done, my children, here are the ingredients," said the grandmother, placing a tray and bowls on the small table with spreadable cheese, grated cheese, ham cut into small pieces, olives, a tomato and a carrot. And so, guided by their grandmother, Jacob and Camila mixed the chopped cooked ham well with the cream cheese and added a little grated cheese to make the mixture firmer. Then they divided everything into three parts that worked with their hands until they got three balls: a larger one for the legs, a little smaller for the body and an even smaller one for the head, just as she and Jo had done friends in the cartoon.

Then they gently passed the balls over the remaining grated Parmesan cheese, covering them entirely and placed the largest ball on the plate first, then the smaller one and on top of the smaller one again. They had a lot of fun decorating the puppet, using half an olive for the hat and small pieces of olive for the jacket buttons. They made the mouth with a slice of tomato and the nose with a piece of carrot. They used a long strip of ham and two sticks made of carrot for the arms as a scarf.

"Wow, it's as beautiful as the cardboard one!" the children exclaimed happily.

"And it's also very good," laughed the grandmother. "Now we have to put it in the fridge to let it cool, and you will see that tomorrow everyone will be amazed."

And so it was. The cheese puppet was a nice and delicious surprise for everyone and brought joy to the table during Christmas lunch. Everyone ate with relish, including Jacob and Camila.

And they learned that, even without snow, you can still have fun, just use your imagination!

Recipe for children: Christmas snowman.

If you want to make the snowman recipe that was described in the story, you need these ingredients:

400g of cream cheese (e.g., Philadelphia) 60g of cooked ham, one tomato, one carrot, some pitted olives q.b. grated Parmesan cheese

You can also use other vegetables as you like to decorate them, such as asparagus, green beans, parsley or chives.

Then leave the puppet in the fridge for at least 4 hours and, before serving, surround the base with crackers, or rocket, or tomato slices.

History of wooden letters.

The story History of the wooden letters is, among fairy tales and stories to soothe children, dedicated to all those who wonder what words are for. When they start to speak of the older children, we think of the little ones, when they begin to feel curiosity towards the written words of adults, when we do not know how to express our feelings clearly, and we would like to communicate with them better. When we read them a fairy tale, the children are helped by the intertwining, at first confused, then increasingly aware, of history and magic, reality and fiction, in their mind.

Before and after the story, we adults can teach them to use words in the right way.

Story to read to children: Story of wooden letters and magic words.

For Christmas, Carter received a magic box. It is a box of toys and, at first, he did not know it was magical. There are also some wooden letters, but Carter doesn't know how to use them. In truth, Carter doesn't really know what letters are. "Dad, what are the letters for?" "They are used to compose the words.

The words we speak and those we write," replies the father. "Can we write with letters?" Asks Carter. "Yes, we can write whatever you want," replies the father. Today Carter is at home; he does not go to kindergarten. He stings her throat, he can't eat, and he can't even drink. His father consoles him, and it is at this point that he comes up with an idea. He takes the wooden letters, puts them next to each other and writes:

"UGLY SORE THROAT."

"See Carter; I wrote UGLY. Then I wrote MAL. I wrote DI. I wrote THROAT. Bad sore throat." Dad, write, "go away, sore throat!" "Okay," says the dad. He takes other letters and writes:

"GO AWAY SORE THROAT."

The child today is really very sick; he has a fever and even a bit of otitis. "Dad, my ears hurt!" The baby cries. "Let's write it down!" Says the father. With other wooden letters, he writes:

"UGLY EAR PAIN."

"Dad, it hasn't passed me yet," says the child. "Can we leave the words you wrote? Will it pass me if we leave the writing?" "It will pass because I gave you the medicine," replies the father. "We, however, leave our little words anyway. We will take them off when you are healed." A day goes by, another day and another day. The wooden letters and magic words remain on the bedroom table because Carter still has a fever, sore throat and earache. On the fourth day, however, Carter recovered. Dad promised that when he is well, he can invite his friend Cora to play with the truck, the doll's room and the toy box. "Dad, I'm healed now. What do we do with the magic words?" "What do you want to do? Shall we put the letters back in place?" "Dad, can I write a message for Cora?" "Sure, she'll see it as soon as she walks into your bedroom. What do we write?" "Dear Cora, play with me. Sore throat, don't come back." "It seems like a nice message to me." Dad takes the wooden letters, turns them over and over and writes:

DEAR CORA, PLAY WITH ME. SORE THROAT, DON'T COME BACK.

The sore throat did not return, and Cora started playing with the wooden letters.

You have another magic to learn: how words are made up.

Marta and Santa's cookies.

That day, on leaving the school, little Marta was happier than usual. She greeted the other companions and teachers, and immediately she got into the car with her father.

It was, in fact, the last day of school before the Christmas holidays, a party that she loved. The family would get together, there would be the tree with the decorations and the many-colored lights and then the nativity scene, the Christmas sweets, the gifts, in short, she couldn't wait for it to all begin! "What a nice dad, it's Christmas in two days!" she exclaimed. "And this year, since you did well, there is also a nice surprise," replied the father. "A surprise? And which?" Marta asked, curious and amazed. "Try to guess," he said, playing to keep her on her toes for a little longer. "I do not know! Come on, pops, tell me! Tell me, come on! " insisted the very curious little girl. "This Christmas we will go on holiday to the mountains with our grandparents," finally answered her father. "Uauuuuu," shrieked the little girl in the height of happiness, "and when do we leave?" "After lunch, Mom is already finishing packing," he smiled at her. "And can we take

Coco with us?" the little girl was suddenly worried. Coco was their little dog of just six months. "Of course," her dad reassured her. As soon as they were home, Coco immediately ran to meet her cheerful and looking for pampering as she always did, and she hugged him, caressed him and scratched his belly. They had become two inseparable playmates. Her mother also met her. "My love, how did you go to school?" she asked her about her, giving her a kiss. "Did Daddy tell you we're going on vacation to our grandparents?" "Yeeeeeeeeeeee, he told me!" Marta screamed, jumping for joy. "Very well, I just finished packing my bags," Mom said. "Can I bring some toys?" she pleaded, "Yes, but two or three at the most because there isn't much space in the trunk. Which would you like to bring?" Mom asked, smiling because she already knew the answer.

"The little mechanic, Princess Paqui and the book of fairy tales," replied the little girl without even thinking about it. They were her pastimes absolutely referenced. Fortunately, although complete with everything, it was a mini mechanic's kit. Marta even wanted to take her on a camping trip last summer, and she enjoyed repairing the table and other objects for the Paqui doll and her little dog. On the other hand, the storybook was essential to make her fall asleep, so her mother said yes and, in a short time, everything was ready for departure: the suitcases, the package with the toys, and even her puppy in the carrier.

The journey by car lasted several hours, but for Marta, they quickly passed between the tales, the Christmas carols and the games played with mom, dad and Coco. Eventually, the little girl, very tired from all the emotions of that long day, fell asleep.

The next day was Christmas Eve. When she woke up, she found herself already in her grandparents' hut and immediately got off her wooden bed to look for them. Coco, who had been sleeping, crouched next to her, ran after her.

"Hey honey, are you awake already? Come here, let us hug you," said the grandmother, who was already in the kitchen preparing her delicious dishes for Christmas Eve. "Would you like to help me make cookies with your mother after breakfast?".

"Yeeeeeeeeeeee granny!" the girl answered enthusiastically. "I also brought my toy tool case, which is made of wood, just like your house; if you have something to repair, I'm here!"

Marta really liked that large wooden house, with the fireplace, always lit in winter. Outside the windows, the landscape, with the mountain and the expanses of fir trees covered with snow, seemed enchanted. It was as if they lived in a world of fairy tales.

They all had breakfast together, then grandfather and dad went out to get wood and grandmother, mom and granddaughter dedicated themselves to sweets. "We will make St. Nicholas' favorite cookies. I prepare them every year, you know? " said the grandmother.

"Who is San Nicola?" asked the child. "Let's see if you guess right," the mother intervened. "He is the saint who protects all children, and every year he brings gifts to the good ones, so is St. Nicholas him?" "But he's Santa Claus!" Marta exclaimed. "Very good! Yes, that's him," the grandmother replied. "And how do you know these are her favorite cookies of hers, Grandma?" the child asked. "Eh, wait and see ..." she said, smiling and winking at her mother.

And so, following the grandmother's recipe, they poured into a large bowl: flour, cold butter cut into small pieces, egg yolks, sugar, vanilla extract, baking powder and grated lemon peel. They mixed everything well until they got a single block. Then they placed it on a floured pastry board and worked it again with their hands until the block became smooth and homogeneous. Then, they rolled out the dough with a rolling pin until it was three or four millimeters high. Then they cut out the dough with molds in the shape of a star, heart, fir and snowman.

The child had a lot of fun with her grandmother next to her, her part of the dough, the rolling pin and the molds to imitate the wise gestures of her grandmother and mother, and she too cut out many cookies. In the end, they placed them on baking sheets lined with baking paper and brushed them with egg white, then sprinkled them with colored pralines or cane sugar and baked at 180 degrees for about 15 minutes.

"Be careful; the biscuits must not take on color, but only cook," warned the grandmother.

When they took them out of the oven, the kitchen filled with a delicious scent; while they were still hot, they made a hole in each cookie with a wooden skewer toothpick, and after a while, when they were well cooled, they passed through each hole in the ribbon and hung them on the Christmas tree along with the other decorations.

"This is the greediest tree I've ever seen!" exclaimed the satisfied mother.
"Me too," joined Marta happily.
"Yes, now it's complete, and it turned out really good!" confirmed the grandmother.

"Wuf!" Coco snorted as a sign of approval as she gnawed on a bone-shaped biscuit made with special ingredients, which the child had prepared just for him.

Gathered for lunch, the little family spent the rest of the day on Christmas Eve cheerfully. In the afternoon, they took the child to play in the snow. In the evening, after a good dinner, they chatted and joked all together in front of the fireplace until late. When the time came, they went to bed, and their father began to read Marta the usual story about her to make her fall asleep.

"It's okay, Dad, I'm already so sleepy," said the little girl. "But you say that Santa Claus will come tonight?" "Have you been good this year?" her father asked her. "Yes, yes!" she exclaimed, quite sure. "He will come for sure. Stay calm and have many beautiful dreams," said her father, kissing her goodnight. She caressed Coco and went to bed too. Despite her tiredness, Marta was unable to sleep right away. She was anxious about Santa's visit. She listened to the slightest noise and trying to figure out if it was he who was descending from the chimney, but in the end, sleep overcame her, and she fell asleep.

The next morning, as soon as she woke up, she immediately got out of bed and ran into the kitchen very excited "Has Santa Claus come? It came?" she screamed with her puppy following her. Everyone was at the table for her breakfast and said good morning. "Hello, baby," said the grandfather.

"Yes, he came! Let's go and see under the tree" They went to see and—surprise!—they found a large package wrapped in colorful Christmas paper together with a note on which was written: "For Marta."

Grandfather took the card and read it aloud for everyone, "Dear Marta, I wanted to thank you for the delicious cookies you made for me. I liked them a lot, you know? I was so tired, cold and hungry when I arrived in this cabin and found so much goodness and so much warmth there. Thanks for warming my heart. I leave you the gift you want so much, and I hug you with great affection. Signed: Santa Claus."

Everyone approved, "Very well, Marta!" "But then it's true that these are her favorite cookies!" The little girl, who was speechless in astonishment, exclaimed. "Yes, that's right," her grandfather smiled. "Come on, unwrap the gift and let's see what it brought you." The child untied the ribbon, eagerly tore off the paper and - uauuu! - Inside, she found a beautiful stroller for her doll, decorated with butterflies and flowers, obviously made of wood too. "It's beautiful!" she screamed and ran to get her Paqui to take her for a walk. Needless to say, Coco also found a place in the stroller while Marta was playing little mother, and from time to time with her tools, she pretended to repair the wheels of the stroller with her tools, happily spending the rest of that holiday, which was unforgettable for her, surrounded by the love of her loved ones.

Recipe for children: Santa Claus cookies.

If you want to make the classic Christmas cookies to hang on the tree, as described in this story, you need these ingredients:

350g of 00 flour, 250g of butter, 4 eggs, 8g of baking powder for cakes, 150g of sugar vanilla extract or the seeds of half a vanilla bean grated rind of a lemon or if you prefer an orange cane sugar q.b. colored pralines q.b.

Note

A tip: before baking them, you can still put the biscuits raw in the fridge for about twenty minutes.

This helps prevent them from turning out during cooking.

Why play by copying the greats?

The mechanic's tool game and the kitchen game are ideal educational games to stimulate learning in children aged 2-3 years and over through the natural imitation of adult gestures. Being in a constant learning phase is, in fact, one of the characteristics of the little ones and both plays and the repetition of what adults do are the means by which they learn more easily, preparing a rich store of knowledge for their future life.

Playing cooking, for example, is great entertainment for all children who have a lot of fun preparing the most imaginative recipes while learning to cut, peel, mix, cook, knead, bake, wash the dishes and then all one series of concrete skills, but not only. During this playful activity, they also experience new situations that help them develop their emotional sphere,

socialization, logical thinking, psychomotor skills.

The toy kitchen, being completely similar to a real kitchen, offers an even more engaging play experience, and if supported by the presence of adults, it becomes, even more, a growth laboratory, just as it was for Marta, the protagonist of this beautiful story, which while playing, learns to prepare delicious Christmas cookies and much more.

Santa's cookies - Martha and the Christmas stars.

Preparation time

45 minutes

Cooking time

15 minutes

Total time

1 hour

If you want to make the classic Christmas cookies to hang on the tree, you will need to buy star-shaped molds of different sizes as described in this story.

Ingredients

350 g of flour 00
250 g of butter
4 eggs
8 g of baking powder for cakes
150 g of sugar
vanilla extract (or the seeds of half a vanilla bean)
the grated rind of a lemon (or an orange if you prefer)
cane sugar q.b.
Colored sprinkles q.b.

Instructions

To prepare poinsettias, start by pouring the flour, the cold butter cut into chunks, the four egg yolks, the sugar, the vanilla seeds, the yeast into a large bowl with grated lemon (or orange, if you prefer) peel.

Mix everything until you get a single block that you will transfer to a pastry board; you will work until you have a smooth and homogeneous mixture.

Roll out the dough with a rolling pin on the floured pastry board and form a 3-4 mm thick sheet.

With the star-shaped molds, obtain many shapes that you will pierce in the center with other star or round molds of smaller dimensions (all the small stars removed from the central part of the biscuits can be kneaded to form other biscuits or bake in a separate pan.

Arrange the biscuits on baking sheets lined with parchment paper, brush them with egg white and sprinkle them with brown sugar or colored or silver sugars, then bake at 180 degrees for about 13-15 minutes; consider that the biscuits must not take on color but only cook.

Let the cookies cool and then pass inside the central hole of each of them, the ribbon or the raffia that you will need to hang them on the Christmas tree.

Note

Tip: before baking them, you can still put the biscuits raw in the fridge for about twenty minutes. This helps prevent them from turning out during cooking.

Stories and magic: reading for children.

Dear parents, the candy to grow up is one of those children's readings that combine stories and magic in a solution that we hope you will enjoy. In many fairy tales for children to read, the spell of growing up or becoming small appears in the tradition; it is a metaphor that children like and evokes the phases of growth and change that they experience day after day. So many questions are crowded behind growing together, for children and adults; what does it mean to grow up? Why does one grow up? Will it be beautiful anyway? For adults, do we really help our children to grow up?

History of candy to grow up.

One day Alice went into her grandmother's bedroom secretly. When she was at her grandmother's house, she always played in the dining room or the kitchen. Grandmother preferred to have Alice always near and said: stay here with me while I cook or knit. Grandma's bedroom, however, had something magical about it. It was all colored pink and brown and smelled different from that of Mom's bedroom. She had a pearl necklace on the wall and lots of photographs on the dresser and boxes and boxes of all kinds. Alice opened them all and in a box, the smallest, she found a pink candy. It smelled good. Alice put it in her mouth and ate it. It was a magical candy, a candy to grow up! Alice transformed; she grew, grew and grew to be very tall. Her head reached the ceiling of the room! How strange to be so big! Alice looked at her hands and legs; she turned her head, right, left, down. How small the objects now seemed! The child then began to walk. She immediately tripped and hurt her foot: it was grandma's bed! How could anyone walk into that room now that Alice was so big?

Meanwhile, the grandmother was calling her, "Alice, Alice, where are you?" "I'm here, grandmother; I'm in the bedroom!" Alice said, but her voice as a grown-up child was different. She had a big voice that her grandmother did not recognize. "You are not Alice; this is not your voice! Are you the candy sorceress?" Where did you hide my granddaughter?" "Grandma, it's me! Come and see; I'm in my room!" The grandmother ran into the bedroom and saw Alice, who had grown very tall. "Alice, what have you done?" Said the grandmother. "I ate the pink candy from the box," the little girl said, embarrassed… "I didn't know it was a candy to grow up! Not so big!" "My child, that's an enchanted sugar that a sorceress gave me. I had kept it for you, but it was still early to give it to you." "How do we do it now, grandmother?" "Take this," said the grandmother, handing Alice a blue candy. Alice ate it and transformed again. Something, however, she went wrong again because she became small, almost like an ant. "Alice, where are you?" Asked the grandmother. "I do not see you!" Tiny Alice was very frightened. A giant shadow was above her and did not show her the ceiling. It was her bed! Alice was small now; she saw the specks of dust under the bed, the gnats flying, and the room seemed to her a huge city. She heard her grandmother and replied, "I'm here, grandma!" But her voice was faint, and her grandmother could not hear it. Alice began to cry. The cry of the children is very strong; this time, her grandmother heard it.

"My little one," said the grandmother. Maybe I got the wrong candy. Now I have to give you another candy to become big, but of the right size. Grandmother rummaged through her boxes and found another magical candy. Larger than the blue candy, smaller than the pink candy. She gave it to Alice, and the little girl ate it. Slowly, the child returned to its initial size. The grandmother's bedroom, the bed, the photographs and everything else was as it was before. "Grandma," Alice cried, and her grandmother hugged her. "Next time, ask me when you want to eat something really good," said the grandmother. "To grow up, children don't need sweets, but pasta!" and they all went into the kitchen for lunch.

Children's readings and road signs.

Dear mothers and fathers, the story about the game of road signs is, among the readings for children, dedicated to our slightly older children, who, as they grow up, become more and more curious and want to know how signage works in cities. From the age of 4 and 5, children, if they walk with us in urban streets, may be intrigued by the signs of "stop," "give way," and so on. Teaching them the signs is the first approach to road education and will help them, as they grow up, to move in urban contexts with greater safety.

Reading for children: Peter, the unknown city and the game of traffic signs.

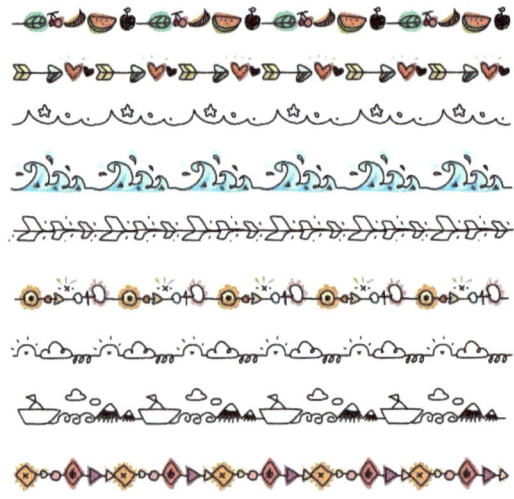

On Peter's eight-year birthday, something strange happened. Growing up with mum, dad and little brother had been nice and fun, but now Peter was big; he had to turn eight! Peter's birthday was August 5th. It was a beautiful summer day and, waiting for the party organized for the afternoon, Peter, with his mother and brother Kyler, had gone to the playground. "Don't go away," said Mom, who was sitting on the bench talking to her friend. "Don't go beyond the blue gate." Now, Peter had a great curiosity to go beyond the blue gate. Younger brother Kyler, who always followed him everywhere, went with him. Beyond the blue gate, which was open, there was a narrow path, very mysterious. The curiosity grew even more because there were some beautiful games at the end of the path; a slide among the highest and a climb to climb that Peter had never seen.

Peter and Kyler ran fast on the path. Mom had said not to go away, so she was sneaking and wanted to be fast. After the trail, however, the playground was no longer visible. Peter found himself in front of a part of the city that he did not know, large, made up of many roads, passing cars and motorcycles, traffic lights. Maybe he had strayed too far. The little brother said, "The high slide! It's back there, Peter. Shall we go there?" The youngest child had a sharp eyesight. The playground was far away. You still had to cross many roads to get there, and Peter didn't know how to do it. He wanted to go, but he was also a little afraid. "Peter, shall we go?", Repeated the little brother, shouting. Peter remembered a traffic sign game he had received as a present the day before. It was a box with toy signs, made of wood, which Peter had pretended not to look at. The first road sign was the traffic light, and everyone knows this. "Kyler, if we want to cross the street, we'll wait for the light in front of us to turn green," Peter said, and they did. They crossed the street, but the second sign was more difficult: it was a triangle with a train symbol. "Peter, look, it's a triangle with a train inside!" Said the little brother. What did Mom say in the traffic sign game about triangles? They were the warning signs! Peter had to make an effort to remember that signal meant a little farther on, there were tracks, and a train could pass. "Ah, now I understand," said Peter, "we have to be careful because a train might pass. They walked a little longer and found themselves in front of some tracks. The little brother wanted to cross them, but Peter stopped him in time. There was a loud sound, the noise of the train on the tracks and shortly after the train passed. As the train passed, the children crossed the level crossing and were faced with another sign. It was a blue circle with a gentleman on foot and a bicycle inside. "Look, Peter, a gentleman walking inside a blue circle," said the little brother. Peter began to think; what did he mean when the signal was a circle? A circle, a circle... "the circle is a sign of obligation." "Kyler, we're safe! Only people on foot and bicycles can pass on that road. Here we go!" The two brothers ran along the road after the blue circle and found themselves at the park of the very high slide. They played until they got tired and then went back, to be found by their mother, carefully observing the signs, as if according to the game of road signs. That day, Kyler had also grown up with his big brother, at least for a little while. Mom said, "Where were you, children? Did you go beyond the blue gate?" "No, mom," they answered in chorus. They had learned the game of traffic signs. They still had to learn the game of "always telling the truth."

When children have a tantrum.

Dear mothers, we know that a child can also become very difficult to manage when there are too many tantrums. For this, we have included, among the fairy tales for children, a story that could be useful to calm the little ones and reassure the grown-ups; the whims end, sooner or later and with a little patience, firmness and a lot of diplomacies, it is possible "negotiate" even with the most stubborn warriors.

Leo's sword when he throws too many tantrums.

Leo is a warrior child, strong and does not accept no. When someone says no to Leo, Leo takes his sword; he fights and always wins. Sometimes Leo argues with his mom. Mum says, "Finish lunch first, then TV," and Leo doesn't want to. She also says, "Put everything in the toy box," and Leo doesn't want to. "Put the wooden puzzle in order, or you'll lose the pieces," and Leo doesn't want to. When Leo does not like something, he takes out his sword; it is a magical sword, invisible, not seen, but it hits very hard. Leo fights with his sword and leaves all games in a mess.

"Leo, get it right," Mom says. "I am a warrior, mom." "I'm fighting with the sword." "Leo, like a good guy," says Mom. "Tidy up, after you can play with the sword."

Mom just doesn't understand. "Leo, don't throw a tantrum. Put it right," says the mother, and she is losing patience a little. If the mother loses her patience, Leo gets even more desire to play with the sword; she has to defeat all the "enemies," and there are many! "Leo, tidy up. I'm telling you for the last time.

Now I'm going to the kitchen; when I get back, I want to see your little room neatly arranged. Mom goes into the kitchen, the phone rings. "Yes, it is. When he throws too many tantrums, Leo is intractable," Mom says on the phone. Leo still has his sword. He must fight against all the enemies he sees. He swings and waves his sword, but at some point, he is so tired that he can no longer make war. Mom has finished her call and is coming back. She has a question mark on her face, "What are you doing?" She asks Leo. "Mom, I am a warrior." "Yes, Leo," Mom says. "What are you doing now, warrior? Where is your sword?" "My sword today has defeated many enemies; it must rest. I support you here."

"Okay," Mom replies. "What do we do with the wooden puzzle and the toys scattered on the ground?" "Mom, will you keep my sword while I put it away?" "Sure," Mom replies with a smile. Leo puts the toy box in place and tidies up the bedroom. "Mom, I'll put the sword in place too. I will fight tomorrow," says the warrior.

Fairy tales for children: the chocolate of calm.

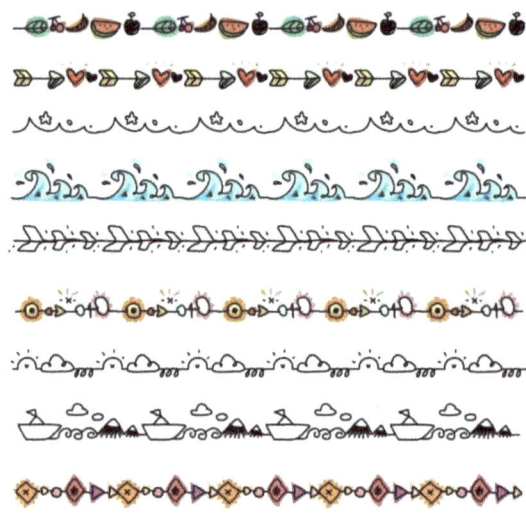

Dear mothers, this children's story is dedicated to our little and big loves that become really difficult to manage when they get angry or have a tantrum. We thought of a recipe, chocolate of calm, a magical drink that, perhaps, would also be good for adults.

Consider this story, among the tales to soothe children, as a humble suggestion to all of us. A hug!

The girl who went on a rampage and the chocolate of calm.

Aria was a beautiful and very good child; only when a game did not turn out well, she became a child who went on a rampage; she fidgeted, got angry, cried, slammed her feet and screamed until she was exhausted.

Her mom said, "Aria, don't be so mad. Come, let's find a solution, your mother is here for you, everything will soon pass," but the little girl was crying, and there was no way to calm her down.

One day Aria was building a tower out of colored plastic building bricks. She had worked hard because she wanted to make it very high, brick by brick… but, in an instant, the tower collapsed, and her pieces ended up everywhere!

Aria went on a rampage; she cried and screamed so much that she woke the fairy of silence.

Aria's mother was in the kitchen washing her dishes; she had decided to leave Aria alone so that she would decide once and for all to end these whims. She saw nothing, not even the fairy of silence, an all-blond lady, whom only children could see.

The fairy of silence said to the child,

"Aria, why are you crying so much?"

"I just cry," Aria said.

"I understand. You cry because you have not yet drunk the chocolate of calm."

"What is the chocolate of calm?" Aria became curious because the word calm, but above all, the word chocolate, interested her greatly.

"It is magical chocolate, which is prepared in a magical cuisine. Do you have a kitchen, Aria?"

"I have a play kitchen, made of wood, which my mother gave me, but it is not magical," replied the child.

"That's what you say," said the fairy. "Tell me where your kitchen is; I'll prepare the ingredients."

The fairy approaches Aria's kitchen; there was a stove, a sink, an oven, a clock to check the time while she cooked. "This is serious," Aria thought and walked over to her, handing her a saucepan and a spoon.

"How is magic chocolate made?" asked the child.

"Here it is," said the fairy of silence, stirring in the saucepan. "We have cocoa, sugar, potato starch... I forgot the milk. Can you take it for me?" Aria also had a wooden fridge between the cabinets in her bedroom. She returned to the fairy with the milk jug, more and more curious. There was nothing in the saucepan; was the fairy pretending, or would a chocolate really arrive? Aria was starting to feel like it.

"Come on, Aria, you mix a little." Aria went to the kitchen and stirred in the saucepan with her spoon. "You have to turn slowly, slowly and count to 10," said the fairy. "Are you sure?" Said the little girl. "I'm sure," said the fairy. They mixed together. 1, 2, 3... the child had learned to count to 10!

The wooden kitchen was truly magical! In the saucepan, she began to see a cream with a good smell. "Taste it," the fairy said to Ira. "It's good," the little girl exclaimed. She had never tried such sweet chocolate. "It is the chocolate of calm. However, you can have it only when you have the patience to mix slowly and count up to 10," explained the fairy.

At that moment, Mom, realizing that Aria was no longer crying, went back to see what had happened.

"Mom, would you like a cup of chocolate?" Asked the little girl. The fairy of silence was gone; Aria, however, was no longer a little girl who went on a rampage because she had the recipe for the chocolate of calm.

Children's fears: a tale to soothe children.

Dear parents, we were inspired by an Italian folk tale for this story, our protagonist is called marabesù, and it is thought to be a bird. We have no images of this legendary animal; some think it is a bird, for others a magical sheep that roam at night in the woods and makes a terrible noise, frightening young and old. In our story, however, the marabesù will reveal his true nature, affable and generous. This story is special because it is part of the reassuring tales to calm children and make them understand that, once fears are overcome, there can be nice surprises, and above all, in every experience, you grow a little.

The marabesù crying in the woods.

"Don't shout, wake up the marabesù!" Grandmother said to the child before going to sleep. The marabesù was told as a frightening animal, which, however, no child in the town had ever seen. Everyone said he looked awful; he could turn into a bird, sometimes he was a bat, sometimes he was an owl, or when he wanted to get close to a house, he turned into a sheep with magical powers. Mom and dad did not believe these stories; all the town elders, however, always said to the children or their grandchildren, "If you have a tantrum, I'll call the marabesù!" and the children trembled with fear. One night a little girl from the village named Ana went to bed frightened and with a troubled heart because she had heard the tale of this legendary animal. Everyone slept, mom, dad, her two brothers, grandparents next door and the dog. The little girl woke up and looked around, it was all dark, and her mother had not yet arrived to say, "Wake up in the morning," and a noise came from the woods. A strange cry, the cry of an animal, but not a known noise, the croaking of a frog or the squawking of a duck, a different noise. It sounded like a knife screeching on stone, falling pots and broken glasses on the floor, all together.

"The marabesù!" Cries the child, "Mom, the marabesù!

Mom woke up and ran into the little girl's room. "There is no one, my love." "The marabesù does not exist, and the forest is silent."

The sound was no longer heard, and Mom kissed Ana on her forehead and went back to her room upstairs. After a while, the little girl heard that strange sound again. "The marabesù! Mom, he's back!" Mum couldn't hear him, it was a summer night, and dad had left a window open, and the woods became silent for a few minutes. The little girl held her breath and hid under the covers, her eyes open. Then she heard a beating of wings and a cry; it resembled the verse from before, but not so loud. The animal took advantage of the open window, entered the house and placed itself on the child's bed. "Hi, little girl," she cried. Ana, frightened, pulled one eye out from under the blanket to look; she was trembling with fear; the marabesù had really arrived!

The grandparents were right; it was a bird, all blue, with bright feathers, not so big in reality, and much less frightening to see up close. Only the sound of her was frightening. The little girl was trembling; even the strange bird trembled.

"Do you know where my mom is?" The animal said to Ana. "I lost it while I was flying in the forest, I saw an open window, and I thought it was here."

The little girl wanted to answer, but her voice remained in her throat, such was her fear. Grandparents used to say that marabesù s kidnap children! This, however, was a puppy and did not seem so dangerous.

"Why don't you answer, child? Did you take my mom?" Said the little bird. In the meantime, in the woods, it seemed that it was day and all the animals were awake; there was a great noise: croaking of frogs, howling of wolves and other sounds in the distance.

The little girl's voice returned slowly. "What is your mom like, bird?" The puppy replied, "It's made just like me, but bigger."

"Bird," continued the little girl. "You are bad? Is your mom bad?" "My mom is not bad!" cried the bird and jumped into a rage. "I'm not bad." "Strange bird," the little girl said again. "Does your mom kidnap children?" This time, however, the puppy of the mysterious animal was even more frightened than the child. "You are bad!" she screamed, "your mom is bad." The wind banged hard against the window. There was another strange verse, very, very strong. A larger bird struggled through the window and landed on the child's bed. It was mother marabesù, and she had come and taken her baby. "Puppy," she shouted, talking to the bird, "where were you? I told you many times that you shouldn't go into houses!" The little girl was silent, quietly silent. "Let's go home, puppy," said Marabesù, mother to her baby and then, turning to the girl.

"Hello child, have good dreams and remember. I'll give you a little secret. I'm not bad! Don't be afraid when you hear my cry in the night. I have to scream because this is how my puppy hears me and doesn't get lost in the woods, as he did last night." Marabesù mother and her son flew out the window.

Ana reassured, she wanted to tell the little secret, and she shouted, "Mom!". Mom got out of bed and went to the little girl's room. "What's still there?", She said yawning. "Mom, I have discovered that marabesù are good animals." "Ah," Mom said, nodding yes. "Go back to sleep now."

And Ana immediately fell asleep happy and with a smile on her lips.

When children have a tantrum.

Dear parents, "the little monkey who always wanted to stay awake" is a well-known story. This fable is dedicated, among the fairy tales for children, to those a little more grown-up who begin to understand and have an approximate notion of time. Usually, at this age, children have a little tantrum before going to sleep. However, in a short time, they will be able to grow and learn how good habits, night and day, can help them feel good and recharge all energy in the night to have a good day when you wake up.

The little monkey who always wanted to stay awake.

Sisi was a little monkey who always threw a tantrum before going to sleep. When evening came, her mother would say to her: "Sisi, look at the sky outside! It's all dark, the sun has long gone to sleep! We have to go to sleep too". Sisi always protested every night, "I don't want to go to bed! I always want to stay awake". Sisi was whimsical about her every night, and her father, her mother, her grandparents all called her "the little monkey who always wanted to stay awake." Each evening, Sisi fell asleep later and later. Mom was about to lose patience with her puppy and would tell her: "If you go to bed so late, it will be difficult to get up in the morning." The little monkey, who always wanted to stay awake, however, did not believe in her mother. One evening, Sisi decided; he wanted to stay up all night because he was too eager to jump, run around the house and invent new games.

Her mother said to her: "Okay, Sisi, for this evening, let's do as you want, since you are not sleepy, do not sleep!". The little monkey who always wanted to stay awake was delighted. First, she jumped on the bed in her room, then went to her mother's bed to do somersaults, then it occurred to her to run a bit between the kitchen, the corridor, and the bathroom and competed with her dad. After that, she thought of taking all her toys out of the closet and scattering them on the floor. She also fought with the stuffed animals: what a mess in her bedroom! Mom and Dad had decided to wait for Sisi to get tired by herself, and they didn't say anything about her, but I looked at her desperately from a distance. The little monkey who always wanted to stay awake played and played again. When she closed her eyes, she was lying on the floor, among stuffed animals and buildings. Mom and Dad put her on the bed and went to sleep. The following day, the sun was already high in the sky; Dad had got up to go to work, and Sisi was asleep. Sisi slept all day: many friends rang the little monkey's door who wanted to stay awake all the time. First came Ted, the rabbit who always ate dear you.

"Knock knock, can I come into the house to play with Sisi?" "Hi Ted," Mom said. "I'm sorry Sisi is still asleep."

After a while, Mimi the cat arrived.

"Knock knock, can I go into the house to play with Sisi? "Hi Mimi," said the mother. "Unfortunately, Sisi is still asleep."

The morning hours passed, and the little monkey who always wanted to stay awake was still asleep. Toby, the little dog, also came:

"Knock knock, can I come into the house to play with Sisi?" "Hi Toby," Mom said. "Sisi is still asleep."

Tapy, the mouse who loved cheese, also passed by, but after dark, Sisi's friends all had to go home to their mothers, take a bath, go to dinner and finally sleep. That sleeper Sisi woke up at dinner time that day. "Where are my friends?" Said Sisi. "They're all home," Mom replied. "Look at the sky, Sisi: it is almost sunset time, the sun is about to go to sleep, and soon it's time for dinner. You woke up too late". "No! It's not late, and I'm Sisi, the little monkey who always wanted to stay awake!". She protested the puppy.

"Sisi," explained Mom, "while you were asleep, your friends were all awake and wanted to play with you. Now you are awake, and you want to play, but it is evening, your friends have gone home, and soon they will go to bed." "No!" Sisi protested again, who did not want to believe his mother. But now she felt alone, and she didn't understand: why was the sun going to sleep? Why was it evening again, and why did she have to listen to the grown-ups? After dinner, the little monkey who always wanted to stay awake didn't want to play. She had been alone all the time, and she felt a little sad. She was bored, but she was not sleepy; it was a nice nuisance to be a little monkey who wanted to stay awake all the time! A few days passed, and Sisi was getting sadder and sadder. Her friends did not come to visit her, and she no longer knew when it was time to go to sleep. "Mom, will you help me fall asleep?" asked the monkey. So her mother started reading her a book, singing her a lullaby and slowly, the little monkey who wanted to stay awake all the time changed. Dad had established a rule: he went to bed right after the stuffed animal fight. After dinner, the father said: "It's time for the plush fight!" and Sisi was having a blast. Afterwards, the father and Sisi put away the soft toys, the mother came to read a story, and Sisi fell asleep. When Sisi learned to fall asleep in time, her friends returned to visit her, and she was happy and content again. She had become the little monkey who slept at night and played a lot during the day, like many monkeys, in all the countries of the world.

Tales for children to grow up together.

Dear parents, this "fox cub who did not listen" reminds us very closely of our little ones of 2 or 3 years of age. We have collected this story, among children's fairy tales, because a mother confessed to us that her puppy loved to hear it often repeated, in the evening, before going to sleep. Maybe the little foxes want to find out what the limit is, between the desire to dare, the risk of disobeying, fear, and doubt about what comes next? Maybe children want to understand how and why to learn to listen to their parents and follow their advice?

Lacky fox cub who did not listen.

Lacky was a fox cub who didn't listen. He was already two and a half years old; he could walk, jump, eat alone, talk. Lacky had learned to go up and down stairs alone, and he was very happy to know how to do all these things without his mother's help. Even though Lacky knew very well how to climb stairs, his mother had told him:

"Puppy, do not climb the ladder alone."

Lacky fox cub wanted to go up and down all the stairs. So, when mom was in another room or bathroom, she went up and down the ladder. He was fast and very good, when his mother came back, she was already on the ground and never fell.

"Lacky listen to me! Do not climb the ladder: you could fall".

Lacky pretended to listen, but he believed what his mom said to him and thought he would never fall.

If mom was at work and her grandmother was at her house, grandmother would say: "Be careful, Lacky! Do not climb the ladder: you could fall ." Lacky went up secretly when his grandmother didn't see him. He was fast and very good and did not fall. Even Aunt Nina always said, "Don't go up the ladder," but

Lacky fox cub who didn't listen to anyone did it anyway.

When Papa Volpe came home in the evening, he would ask the puppy: "How did it go today? Were you good? Did you listen to your mother?" Lacky always said yes: because no one had seen him go up the stairs. Even grandfather Volpe always told him: "Don't climb the ladder! It's dangerous!". Lacky was a fox cub who did not listen: he had climbed many times and had never fallen! Why was everyone afraid of him falling down the stairs? One day the fox cub was at home with mom. Mom went to the kitchen to cook, and Lacky found a way to play up and down the ladder. However, this time, he put his foot wrong as he got off, tripped and hurt his knee. "Mum, mum! Run!

I hurt myself!" Mom ran to the puppy. She was crying. She wept and cried, and her mother comforted him for a long time. When the pain passed, Mom asked, "Lacky, how did this happen? Where did you fall?" The fox cub told everything. He was coming down the ladder and had fallen. Lacky thought he would never fall down the stairs. "Bratty puppy!" Said the mother. "I told you not to do the ladder alone! Have you seen, now, what can happen?" "Yes, Mom," Lacky said disconsolately because he finally understood.

Stories for children; growing together with the rules.

Dear mothers, "school without rules" is one of those stories for children growing up and who need to understand how and why it is important to learn to follow the rules. Sometimes, it is difficult for us adults to explain everything; it is easy to be tempted to say, "just do it like this," but growing up and learning to obey, you need to understand why. The rules were not born to get in the way, even when they seem so; they were born to help us live better in the community.

The school without rules and the school with too many rules.

The rules chased the baby Daniel all over the place. At the nursery, there had been the rules; at the kindergarten, there were rules. At home with mom and dad, there were rules, and there were even rules from grandparents.

And above all these "blessed rules" were boring, because they were almost always the same everywhere. However, in some places, the rules were slightly different, for example: why could you eat sweets at the grandmother's place and at home with mom and dad?

At school, a sign said:

- I put away the games - I throw the rubbish in the bin - I don't shout - I don't argue - I listen to the teacher.

However, one thing was clear: Daniel didn't like rules. The grown-ups had made them, and he wanted to decide everything himself. One day Daniel thought: "I want to go to a kindergarten where there are no rules." The wish fairy passed by at that moment; he listened to him and decided to please him.

Daniel found himself alone, without his mother, in a kindergarten full of toys. His friends were all with him, which was the "crazy" school because it had no rules to respect.

Since the rules sign was gone, they ran after each other to have a big party. They took out all the toys from the shelves and kept running, jumping, playing without putting anything in place. They were so excited that they shouted all the time; there was no longer any rule to disturb them! The teachers weren't there; they would have been useless in that school because you didn't have to listen to them! Lunch arrived, the canteen service worked, even in the school without rules and the children were all happy because, that day, the menu included a large plate of fries and orange soda. After they finished eating, the children threw their dishes in the air and laughed at each other. There were also candies; Daniel had never seen so many, not even at his grandmother's place. Since, in the unregulated school, there was no obligation to throw litter and food waste in the bin, at one point, Daniel happened to slip on a candy paper and hit his friend Paco with his head. Angela, the youngest girl in the class, was also about to slip on another paper on the ground. Daniel shouted, "Angela, watch out!" But there was too much noise because all the children were screaming and you couldn't hear anything. When all the children were too tired and agitated, some began to cry;

someone jumped and ran out into the garden; many fell asleep. Daniel had eaten too much candy and had a stomach ache.

The whimsical fairy passed by at that moment, and she decided to spite all the children. He took them away from the school without rules, magically, made them arrive in the school of too many rules. There was a very long sign before entering the school of too many rules, and there were no drawings to explain the rules to children who could not read. A teacher who the children did not know came and began to read the rules:

- **I can't run, scream and eat candy**
- **I cannot make bubbles in the glass of water**
- **There is no orange juice**
- **I can't eat with my hands**

- **I can't play in the garden**
- **I can't get my shirt dirty with gravy**
- **I can't sing, because it would be like screaming**
- **I can't get out of my chair**
- **I can't leave food on my plate, even when I really don't like it or it's too much**

The list was so long that the teacher never finished reading. The children were silent and did not dare to move. Daniel had not understood anything: not even a rule for him remained in the lead. He was right; the rules were bad. The teacher, however, continued to read, and there was no way of making her stop. Paco, Daniel's best friend, raised his hand. "Teacher, what are the most important rules?" The teacher stopped reading. She didn't know what to answer, and she had a surprised, very surprised face. No child had asked him such a question. Suddenly, his wish fairy returned. Daniel and all his classmates found themselves in the usual kindergarten, with the sign hanging on the door with only five rules. "Thank goodness," thought Paco, who nodded to Daniel that he was finally calm and went to class happily because now he knew what to do.

History and magic.

Dear parents, that of the golden fish is a Russian fairy tale, written by Aleksandr Pushkin: it came to mind about magic and desires. Let's tell it to our children, among fairy tales, to go to sleep, to distract them or reassure them after a whim and to teach them not to ask too much. Let's remember it in fairy tales to calm children, and let's keep it in mind as adults when we neglect to think that arrogance, presumption, and greed are the whims of adults.

History and magic: The magic of the goldfish.

In the morning, the poor old fisherman leaves the house. He hopes to be able to catch, even today, those few fish that are enough to feed him and his wife. He goes fishing and, suddenly, the net becomes very heavy; inside, there is only a small golden fish. "Let me go, old fisherman! In return, I will magically give you everything you want!" "I want nothing, dear little fish," says the old man, who is humble and good. "Go ahead," and he frees him from the net. When the old fisherman returns home, he tells everything to his wife, the goldfish left in the net, the promise of magic to make a wish come true. "Go back to the little fish, old man," says his wife, shouting. "You have lost an opportunity! Ask him for a new tub; ours is old and worn out." The old fisherman returns to the sea and calls the goldfish.

"Dear little fish, my wife scolded me. We have a completely broken bucket; it is a worn-out wooden bucket. Could you get me a new tub?" "You have been good to me, fisherman. Do not worry. You will have a new tub."

The old man returns home and finds that his wife's wish has come true: she has a beautiful new wooden tub! The goldfish was right. His wife, however, is not happy, "Old fool! You are satisfied with a wooden basin! The goldfish is magical; we can have much more! Go back to the sea and ask him for a big new house!" The fisherman returns to the sea and calls the goldfish.

"Dear little fish, my wife, does not give me peace. She wants a new home" "Don't worry, old man. You will have what you want." The fisherman sets out for home, and when he arrives, he does not recognize it; instead of the ramshackle hut, there is a large house with solid white walls. "We can be happy now," says the fisherman. "Old fool," shouts his wife. "Having a new house is not enough for me; I want to be very rich." "Go back to the goldfish and ask him for gold coins, jewels, stones, and diamonds." The fisherman is sad, her wife asks for more and more, and she is never happy. With downcast eyes, he goes back to the sea and calls the golden fish. "Little fish, my wife can't be happy; she always complains; she wants gold coins, jewels, stones, and diamonds." The goldfish makes a strange face, then a smile. "Okay, old man. Go home, and don't worry."

At home, the fisherman discovers that the magic has come true once again. His wife is well dressed; she has a pearl necklace around her neck, precious rings on her fingers, sitting in front of a set table, and a chest of gold coins next to her. The old woman, however, is not happy and is increasingly capricious. "I'm not happy, old man!" "I want to be empress! Run to the little fish." The old fisherman tries to answer. "We can be happy now." "Go to the magic fish, or I'll have my servants take you away!" Commands the woman. The fisherman returns to the sea and calls the little fish. He is ashamed but asks: "Goldfish, my wife sends me to ask you to make her an empress." The goldfish no longer smiles. "Go home, old man," he says to the fisherman.

The fisherman returns home: the magic has come true, but his wife is increasingly insolent. "I want to be the goddess of the sea!" She shouts at her husband. The fisherman returns to the goldfish.

"My wife wants to be the goddess of the sea," he says. The little fish looks at him for a moment, then is silent and runs away.

The old fisherman sets out for home. However, the big new house has disappeared: the gold coins, the jewels, the new tub have disappeared. His old ramshackle hut is back, and his wife has the worn and worn clothes of the past. "We could have been happy," the old man says to his wife.

Children's stories to read about naughty children.

Dear mothers, who is Aladdin, the naughty child of this story? You will remember, Aladdin is the name of a famous story from The Thousand and One Nights, perhaps among the most beautiful fairy tales for adults and children in literature. The first part of Aladdin's inspires our story; it talks about whims, rules to be respected, spells and behaviors that can change. We choose this one, among children's fairy tales, when we want to remind them that children are not always brats and do not always have a tantrum.

Fable about the whims of children; Aladdin child brat.

Aladdin is a child who throws a tantrum. He is often agitated; he protests when mom and dad says "No" to his desire for him and starts stamping his feet. He cries, complains, screams, and all the neighbors would say,

"Aladdin, stop having a tantrum." Aladdin does not stop. Months go by, even years, and the capricious child becomes a naughty child. Mom, dad, and neighbors would say, "Aladdin, stop being a brat." Aladdin does not stop.

Aladdin often does not obey. When he doesn't obey, his mother says:

"You have to respect the rules; I respect the rules, you respect the rules!" Aladdin then asks his mother, "Do we all have to respect the rule?" "Yes," Mom says. Aladdin protests all the same.

One day a strange gentleman arrives in Aladdin's village and knocks on Aladdin's door. Mom and dad are not there; there is only Aladdin. "Hi," says the gentleman, "I'm looking for a naughty child named Aladdin."

"It's me," Aladdin replies. "Good. I want to make you a very lucky man, "says the gentleman. "I'm not lucky," Aladdin replies. "I am capricious and disobedient." "I know," says the gentleman, "but I want to take you to a place. There is a cave with a treasure; will you help me get it?" Aladdin answers yes. A treasure is a tempting proposition! So the lord and Aladdin go out together and arrive at the entrance to the cave. "Listen," says the strange gentleman, "You will have all the treasure if you go in alone and obey everything I tell you." Aladdin must enter alone! He overcomes his fear of the dark, only to have the treasure… but, once inside, the Lord commands: "Now pass me all the treasure, but stay in the cave. I will only let you out later! ". Aladdin, however, does not obey, and above all, he does not understand: he wants to get out of the cave immediately, and now he no longer trusts this strange gentleman. "Listen," says Aladdin, "I will give you the treasure after I'm come out of the cave." "No," says the gentleman. "Obey, Aladdin! Treasure first, you'll come out of the cave when I tell you."

The lord is, in reality, an evil wizard; he wants to leave the boy alone in the cave, lock him inside with a stone and take all the treasure.

Aladdin does not want to obey. "Sir," asks the boy. "Why do I have to do as you say? Can you explain this rule to me? Do you respect the rules of the village?" "What a rule!" Says the Lord, who is an evil wizard and knows nothing of the village rules. "Obey Aladdin, give me the treasure." Aladdin, then, understands. That gentleman wants to deceive him: he doesn't speak as his mother speaks, and he doesn't know the rules. He comes out of the cave with a leap and starts running, and leaves the strange lord and the treasure behind him. Aladdin runs fast. The magician, in anger, falls into the cave and never goes out. Aladdin is delighted to have returned home to his mother and asks her: "Can you explain the rules to me again?". Since then, he hasn't been having a tantrum and is no longer a naughty child.

Legends and popular stories.

Good evening mothers, this is the tale of "Martin and the bear".

This children's story plays on two common elements in many legends and folk tales: a large animal, which can be a danger to people, children's fear of being out of the house, fear of parents, of losing children.

Fortunately, however, as in many fairy tales, everything ends well.

Martin and the big bear.

Martin was a very intelligent seven-year-old boy. One day of celebration, the boy asked his parents for permission to go to the woods to pick berries. Suddenly, he jumped out a bear, took Martin, caught him, and quickly went to his house. The child was very frightened, but the bear told him: "Don't cry, child. I don't want to eat you, and I won't hurt you. I feel alone; that's why you will stay with me and keep me company." Martin and the bear, therefore, lived together for a while. The bear made him a bed of straw, fed him fruits, berries and honey and treated him with affection. Martin, however, was sad, and he wanted to go home. "Why are you crying, baby?", Asked the bear. Martin was very smart and did not want to tell the bear the truth, so he replied like this, "I cry for my parents since I didn't come home, they will think for sure that you ate me." "Okay," replied the bear. "I'll go to your parents and tell them you're okay, and you will continue to live with me to keep me company." "Cook some sweets to give to your mom; I'll take them in a basket."

Martin agreed but added:

"Desserts are for Mom. You won't have to touch anything from the basket. If you disobey, I will see you ". Martin was a very smart child. He prepared a very large basket, slipped inside, and covered himself with a kitchen cloth. The bear did not notice anything. He took the basket and walked into the woods. In this way, Martin and the bear went to the village together: the bear with the basket in his hand and the child hidden inside. The bear, having reached halfway, muttered aloud: "How heavy this basket weighs, I'll sit down for a minute to rest and eat a cake." Martin, inside the basket, heard everything and whispered, "I see you. Don't eat my mom's sweets." The bear did not see that the child was inside the basket, but heard his voice and was frightened, he added aloud.

"What eyes that child has! He can still see me." He thought that the child was watching him from afar!

And for this reason, the big animal gave up eating sweets. After a while, the bear tried again to say: "Now I'm far away, the child won't see me if I taste some sweets." Martin heard everything, and before the bear could open the basket, he whispered:

"I see you, I see you! Don't eat my mom's sweets!"

The bear gave up eating. Martin and the bear arrive in the village, near the home of the child's parents. Having smelled the bear, all the dogs in the village started barking and running towards Martin's house. The bear was frightened, dropped the basket and fled into the woods. So it was that Martin returned home; he jumped out of the basket still full of sweets and hugged his mom and dad. When the bear returned to his home, he discovered that the baby was not there! After a week, the animal returned to the village to visit the child. The parents were afraid that the bear would kidnap him again, but the animal said: "I have come to greet you because I am leaving for a long journey. Martin, thank you for keeping me company when you were at home with me. I forgive you for deceiving me. You were very clever! I want to leave you a gift that would remind you of me ", he said again and ran away, placing a leather bag on the table; in the bag, there were many gold and silver coins.

Martin's parents built a bigger and more beautiful house with these coins and never forgot the good bear. This story is very popular with children, the story of Martin and the bear; Martin is a smart and likable child who learns to get alone, and the bear is a great good animal.

The metaphor of the rainbow.

Dear mothers, you are about to read a children's fairy tale inspired by a Mayan myth. Ancient peoples had legends and tales designed to explain the origin of the world and the universe; in one of their stories, we found a fascinating metaphor to describe how the rainbow was formed. The rainbow is a bridge between the earth and the sky: the following text, between the fairy tales to calm the children and remedy their fears, is a way to remember that the mother, even when she is absent, returns.

How the rainbow was formed.

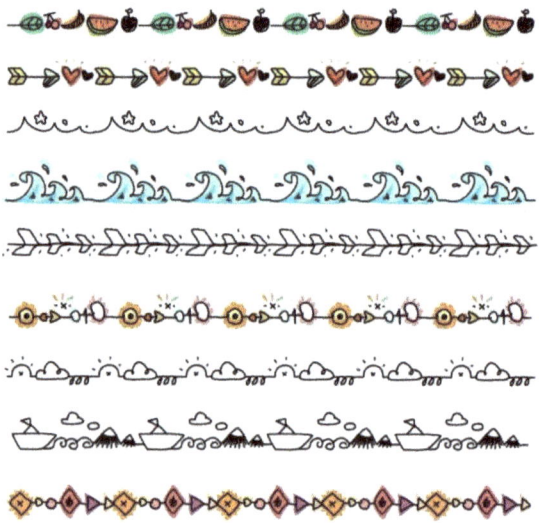

My mom was the goddess of the sky, and she was called Ari. Dad was called Ati, and he was the god of the sea. Their baby was called Tib. They lived on the edge of the earth, in a house suspended between the sky and the sea. Ari and Tib never separated; they were always together, day and night. They bathed in the sea, ate together, slept, and played on the grass. Ati, who happened to be my Dad, slept and ate with them; in the morning, he left the house and returned after a while. Mom used to say, "Dad went to work; he'll be back soon when the sun goes down." Ati had to watch the waters, check the fish, and ensured that the sea animals had food; he also protected the sailors and ships. Tib was very young then, and he didn't understand too well, so he often forgot things so quickly, but he remembered that Dad was home again that evening.

Months passed, and Tib grew. He had learned so many things and understood what happened in the morning after breakfast; Dad went to work, and mom stayed with him to play.

In the last few days, however, her mother was always a bit busy, and she had called a lady to help her: her name was Tati, she was as good as her mother, but she was not her mother. One morning Tati came earlier than usual. Mom got dressed quickly, hugged her baby tightly, and said:

"Today, I will go to work, and you will stay with Tati. I'll be back soon," and she ran away.

Mom was the goddess of the sky, and she also had work to do, such as: directing the rain clouds, controlling the winds, protecting the birds etc.

But Tib didn't understand well. Dad went to work, and so did Mom go to work too? Where was the mother's workplace? Would Mom be back? What did she mean by "I'll be back soon?"

Tib started crying because he was very little and could not understand much. When he cried, the sea below his house became all gray. The fog covered the blue of the sky, and that house no longer seemed happy. Tatì consoled the child and said: "Tib, mother is coming back," but Tib did not believe it; he cried and cried desperately. Why had Mom gone to work? When she cried too much, a blackbird flew near Tib; it was Fear. Fear knew that mother would never come back, and as such, father would also never come back; hence, the house suspended between sky and the sea was no longer there. Since her mother had gone to check the sky somewhere else, a storm broke out near the suspended house; it was Tib's tears that he could no longer stop.

Across the sky, Mom was about to finish the job. After so many months spent at home with her baby, it was her first day, and she no longer found the way she used to be. She traced another path from the ends of the earth to the hanging house. She first crossed the forest, and some of her green colors remained on her clothes. She was about to set the sun, so her mother made a fire to warm herself before continuing, and the orange and red of the fire mixed with the green. The violet of the sunset mingled again.

Mom, walking and walking, left a trail of colors behind her and created the rainbow. In the hanging house, when Tib stopped crying, she saw a bridge between the earth and the colorful sky. Soon after, she saw Mom! She was back, and the bird known as Fear ran away without being seen.

To the children who lived on earth, mothers tell this story to explain how the rainbow was formed. It happens every time little Tib cries too much because mum is not with him, and then mum goes through the forest and creates a bridge to get home.

Children's fairy tales and legends.

A legend tells that the toy benches are all part of the same family: they were carved by fairies and can be found in every home where there is a child. Dear mothers, the following is one of those tales to calm children when they are sad or agitated because they are afraid of leaving a place or a situation they know and are about to face a new experience or a big change.

The game bench.

Ellie had a magical chest. She was in her bedroom, near the soft toys, the bed, the wardrobe, and the shelves with the colors, in the brightest spot in her room. A fairy made this toy bench, but Ellie didn't know.

One day, Mom and Dad told Ellie that they had to move. Furniture, toys, and clothes had ended up in boxes, and a large truck would take them to the new house.

Ellie didn't want to go to the new house.

She liked the old house so much, which she knew well; she knew where her games were, where her mother put the breakfast cookies, and where she hid the chocolate. While her mother was preparing the boxes during the move, Ellie was whimpering, "I don't want to go to the new house!"

Her mother tried to console the child, telling her that everything that ended up in the boxes, including the toys, would be transported to the new house and that nothing would be lost.

One thing, however, had to remain in the old house. The wooden toy chest, because it was fixed to the wall, it just couldn't be transported and had to be left there.

"I want my chest!" Ellie said. "We just can't, baby," replied her mother, "Your bedroom in the new house will be more beautiful than this one."

The child could not regain herself. While Mom was busy closing other boxes, the toy bench, which was magical, she spoke. "Ssssshhh, dear child," she whispered, "Don't worry, because, in every house where there is a child, there is a chest."

"Mom says I have to leave you here!" Ellie said, crying.

"Listen," said the chest, "you'll see that you and I will meet again. Trust me, take out all the toys and leave just one. If you have faith, you will find it again!" Ellie didn't understand the game bench very well. The tone, however, was convincing, and so the little girl emptied the chest of all the bulky toys, and she left, after all, only a puppet, which she used a lot when she was younger. The day of the move came, and all the furniture and boxes were brought into the new house. Ellie's bedroom was the first to be ready; the furniture was assembled quickly, the bed, the wardrobe, and the dressers for the little girl's clothes. Ellie looked around warily because she was still convinced that the old house was better and more beautiful than the new one. Suddenly, however, she noticed that there was a chest between the wardrobe and the desk. Slowly, Ellie approached. Yes, the play bench was very similar to that of the other house. However, it had a different design carved into the wood and was a little larger.

The benches for the toys are all brothers and sisters and are all made by fairies; however, Ellie still did not know this.

"Hi, Ellie," said the bench. "I'm the sister of the chest you left in the old house. Have you noticed that I'm a little older?

You have grown up, and you will need more space for games." The little girl was a little surprised. Were the two benches really sisters? But she remembered very well the puppet she had left on the old bench. With a little fear, she opened the new chest: it was very large and almost completely empty, but at the bottom, there was her puppet when she was little! The puppet she had left in the old house! The toy chest had kept her promise. Ellie was now happy even in the new house!

Children's tales about lacing.

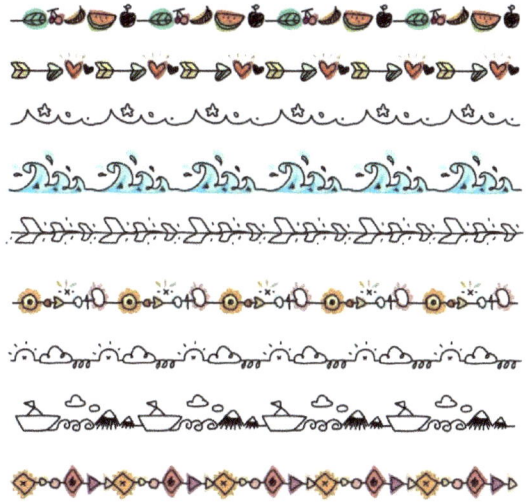

Dear mothers, this children's tale about lacing is dedicated to little ones aged three and up. There is an age to learn how to dress, an age to start putting on shoes, closing them with Velcro, buttoning or unbuttoning a sweater, zipping up a sweatshirt, and finally, fastening. In the land of lacing, our children can, above all, learn to be patient, not lose their temper when they do not know how to perform a task, accept having to make many attempts before succeeding.

The strange land of lacing.

ㅇㅇᢒᨆᢒᨆᢒᨆᢒᨆᢒᨆ

Ricardo had never been to the land of lacing. In truth, Ricardo was a child who didn't know how to tie his shoes; he didn't even know how to button his sweater and zip up his anorak. Every time he tried to buckle up, every time he wanted to zip his sweatshirt alone or undo the buttons on his vest, he constantly failed,

Ricardo tried but couldn't, and finally, he whimpered furiously.

"Ugh." "I don't want to see buttons, zippers, shoelaces, cords in my pants anymore!" He thought.

One day Ricardo had a great misfortune. He was trying to button a cardigan himself when one of the buttons came off the sweater and rolled to the floor. The baby and the mother bent down to pick up the button, but the brat must have gone a long way off because he seemed to have disappeared. The mother and child looked under the sofa, under the table, in the play corner near the coffee table and chest but couldn't see anything. Ricardo saw the button still rolling near the balcony and said: "Mom, come on, the button is running!"

Ricardo and his mother approached the button, tried to grab it, and suddenly the button took off.

It began to fly high in the sky and, magically, Ricardo, and his mother also managed to fly! They clung to the thread of the sweater, which had remained attached to the button, and found themselves high in the sky. The button led them to the land of lacing, there was a sign at the entrance, embroidered with shoelaces, and it said:

WELCOME TO THE COUNTRY OF LACES

This country was very strange; some cloth carpets were held together by some ropes on the pavements. When you arrived at a crossroads with traffic lights and pedestrian crossings, right there, the knots that had been tied to the ropes untied and had to be re-tied to pass. Once they were re-connected, the green light went off! On the stairways, there were new carpets with snaps. It was enough to step on them, with slight pressure, to attach the buttons!. The land of lacing was like this, an immense open-air school where only those who knew how to tie could stay.

"Mom, how will I do now?" Said Ricardo frightened. "Don't worry, my son." "I will help you, and you will learn how to tie shoes, tie knots, button, and unbutton yourself." Mom, therefore, took care of fastening in the most difficult points: at gates and doors, where the knot had to be tied, as in tennis shoes. Ricardo began to practice on easier points; on the stairs, on the elevator buttons, where there were buttons with very large buttonholes, there were strange threads to try and put into the holes in front of the bus stop. This was almost a fun game.

But how did mom and the baby ended up in the land of lacing? When would they get home?

Perhaps the spell was linked to the button that had escaped from the cardigan. Ricardo asked his mother, "Where is the button that flew off? We have to find him and bring him home! " Mom replied, "Let's look for him. The button brought us here, and the button will bring us back." Trying and trying the lacing again, Ricardo and Mom saw their button down the street. You had to cross a bridge to reach it, but it was all made of threads that had to be knotted and tied. Ricardo tried and tried again. Sometimes he succeeded at the first stroke; other times, he whimpered, in the most difficult points, his mother intervened.

The magic button cried out:

"Ricardo's mom! Don't help your child anymore. When he does it all by himself, the bridge will be complete."

Ricardo tried many times. Finally, he was able to thread all the strings, the bridge was ready, and the child could grab his button. Once the button was found, the mother and baby magically returned home. Ricardo had learned to tie shoes, to button and close a zip, but, above all, he knew that what one had to do is to learn, try many times and not lose heart.

Mom had learned that if she wanted to help her son, she had to let him make mistakes on his own!

Didactic fable for children.

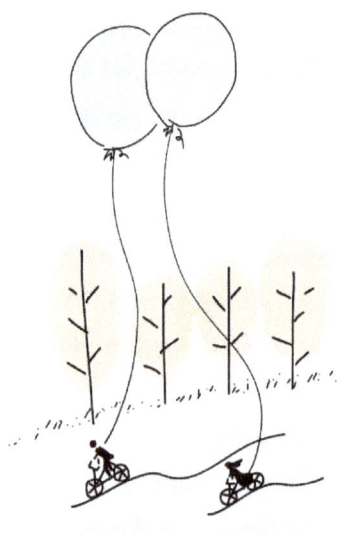

Dear parents, among the children's stories, we found a story on a didactic clock. This fable can be useful for young and old alike. Learning to read the hours on a clock face is no easy task. It is even more difficult for a child to understand what goes on in the heads of adults and what this mysterious, fleeting sense of time is.

Eli, the didactic clock.

Eli was an elephant-shaped didactic clock. It was a simple wooden clock with an elephant drawn near the hands. Eli was a didactic game - they called it that at the store - and it had to be useful for children who wanted to learn to read the hours. The toy had arrived at the home of Tomas, a small child, a bit capricious. Tomas had said, "I don't like elephants!" So Eli was left hanging on his bedroom wall, but no one ever paid attention to it. Nobody used it as a didactic watch, and Eli felt a little lonely.

Meanwhile, Tomas was growing up, and one day he started going to kindergarten. Thus, it was then that the child was faced with a mystery: the watches. Tomas just didn't know how those strange circles that always looked at mom and dad worked.

"Wake up; it's late!". "Hurry up, we have to go to kindergarten." "Turn off that TV; you've been watching it for half an hour!" "It's already nine in the evening, go to bed!" What were all these numbers that made moms nervous? Tomas did not understand. In the morning, he would have liked to play with his toy cars, and instead, he had to have breakfast because it was late. Immediately after breakfast, Mom would immediately say, "let's brush our teeth and face quickly," but Tomas wanted to play a little more, even with the toothbrush. Why did you have to put on your shoes and jacket so quickly? What exactly did he mean, "it's late, we don't have time?"

What was this time? Sometimes Mom would say, "We can't go and buy cookies now; we'll go in the afternoon," but when would the afternoon come? When was dinner time? How did you know when it was late and when it was early?

As Tomas kept asking questions about the weather, Mom thought of asking Eli for help. She took the didactic clock, gave it a good dusting, and instead of leaving it hanging, alone, on the wall, she started showing it to the child. "See," said the mother, moving the shorthand to number 7. "At this time, we get up in the morning. When it is 8 o'clock - the mother moved the shorthand again - we must be in kindergarten. When the shorthand is on 3, and the long hand is on 9, I will come and pick you up from kindergarten. Tomas didn't understand anything at all. He only said: "I don't like elephants" and, capriciously, he turned his head away. Mom smiled slightly and said: "I'll go into the kitchen for a second, look at your watch for a while, and we'll talk about it later." When Mom left, Eli started talking. "Hi, Tomas, we can finally play together." "I don't play with elephants!" Tomas said, still frowning. To himself, he thought: How do wooden toys talk? Eli said: "They are a didactic watch, a bit magical. I teach children how to read the hours" "I already know how to read the hours," Tomas replied, telling a lie out of pure spite. "Okay," Eli said. "Then I'll explain how my dial works. The shorthand indicates the hours. The long hand indicates the minutes." "I don't want to know anything about your hands!" Tomas said, exasperated and red in the face. "I want to know something else. Why does mom always say it's late? Why do I have to go to kindergarten? Why can't I play after breakfast? Above all, what is time?"

Eli was a very patient didactic game. He took a deep breath and looked Tomas in his eyes. "Time is like sand, baby. It is easy to take in hand, but it is also easy to disperse. When they don't know how to hold back time, mothers get upset and worry, they fail to hold sand in their hands, and then time slips even faster ".

Now I'll explain, Eli continued patiently:

"When the short hand points to the number 7, Mom comes to wake you up. Ask her for a second hug ". When the short hand points to the number 8, you will already be in kindergarten. Mom will give you a kiss to say goodbye! When the short hand points to the number 3 and the long hand points to 9, Mom will pick you up at the kindergarten, and you can run to the park!

This was how Tomas learned to read the hours. "Another accomplishment's done, another happy child, "thought the clock.

Fable about children's fears.

Dear parents, we dedicate this fairy tale to the little ones who are afraid of the dark and to all the frightened puppies. Do you remember when as a child, you were afraid of something? You would have wanted a method to make the fear go away, right? Among the children's stories that we propose, this is to be read calmly, many times, close to a reassuring light.

The puppy who was afraid of the dark.

Foncho was a cub bear who was afraid of the dark. He lived in a small house in a clearing near the beginning of the Great Wood together with mum and dad. Dad and mom went to work in the morning and Foncho stayed to play with his friend Luna, a little bear girl, a little older than Foncho and could look after him. Foncho and Luna had a lot of fun together and played all day. Foncho had a desire for some time; he wanted to enter the

Great Wood and overcome his fear of the dark. The Great Wood was so called because fronds, grass and bushes were so numerous that they almost formed a roof over the head of those passing by. Even in the middle of the afternoon, when the sun was still high, it was very dark inside the Great Wood. There was a well-marked path in the woods that Foncho had walked a few times with his mother. The first stretch was bright; afterwards, it was very dark and afterwards, a clearing opened where the sweetest wild blackberries of all grew.

Foncho wanted to pick up the blackberries and take them to mum and dad to eat them all together in the evening, but Foncho was a puppy who was afraid of the dark. How would he have done him? One day her mother gave her teddy bear a present.

"Foncho, this is a flashlight. I know you are a little afraid when it is dark. Always keep it with you on the path."

The bear cub was delighted: he would go into the woods to the blackberry bush! He wanted to surprise Mom and bring her lots of sweet berries to put in the jam.

One day the puppy who was afraid of the dark took courage and walked, with Luna, into the Great Wood. In the beginning, the path could be seen very well because it was still morning and the trees were few. Luna knew the way to the blackberry clearing well; Foncho had her flashlight with him. Soon, however, Foncho and Luna reached that part of the path where the wood was becoming denser. The trees were getting thicker and their branches covered the sky. The puppy who was afraid of the dark stopped. "Let's go home, Luna! I'm afraid!" He said, scared. "Foncho, you wanted to get to the blackberry clearing, right?" Foncho was so afraid. Nothing else mattered. "Let's go home, Luna!" He repeated to him and couldn't say anything else. He was also crying a little. "Foncho, try to turn on the flashlight!" The puppy was so scared that he couldn't do anything. He held the flashlight in his hand, but he didn't turn it on. He just cried and said, "Let's go home!" Luna said: "Can I turn on the flashlight?" Foncho, however, did not want to know. He would have liked to go it alone and would not take advice, but he had tears in his eyes. The puppy tried to turn on the flashlight: he tried, but the flashlight didn't turn on!

Terrified foncho cried more and more. Luna was about to give up the blackberries and said, "Okay, Foncho, let's go back one more time to get the blackberries. Now let's go home; who knows how mom would have been happy." "No!" shouted Foncho. "I want blackberries!" . He screamed and screamed again and tried crying again, but he realized the tears were gone. When his eyes were dry, the puppy, who was afraid of the dark, found himself staring at the flashlight again. Tapping and tapping with his hand, he found the button to turn it on and pushed it right. The flashlight shone! A funny light, which looked like a circle that moved just like Foncho moved his arm up, down, on Luna's face! Foncho also discovered that, with the torch, there was enough light to follow the path. With Luna's help, he went to the blackberry clearing, gathered lots of wild fruits for his mother and returned to the path, lighting it up with the torch. "Mom, we got the blackberries!" He beamed to his mother that evening.

Children's story to read before going to sleep.

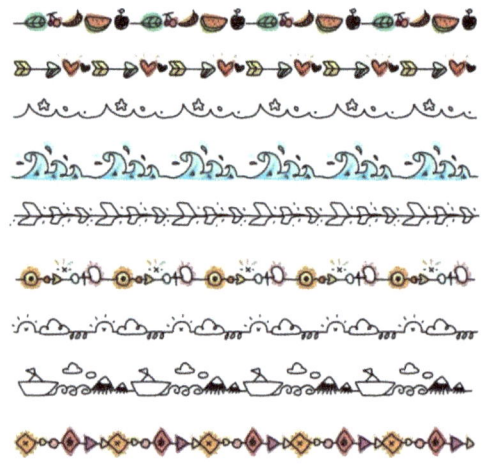

Dear mothers, the next is one of those fairy tales for children to tell in the evening before going to sleep. It is dedicated to children who do not want to go to bed and invent many excuses to postpone the moment of sleep. The story is inspired by a fairy tale of Scottish origin. We have changed the ending, avoiding the elements that could scare the little ones and thinking of a fairy tale to calm the children and bring them, in a sweet sweet way, to the moment of sleep.

Edwin was a child who did not want to go to sleep.

He lived in Scotland, in a stone house on the edge of the country. In the evening, when it was dark and cold outside, Edwinhe stood in front of the fireplace, listening to the fairy tales that his mother told and looking at the fire. When it was time to go to sleep, his mother said, "Now it's time to go to bed,

Edwin", but the little one protested and invented a thousand games to stay awake. One evening his mother, tired of the child's complaints, said to him,

"Okay, Edwin. If you don't want to go upstairs to sleep, stay here. It will mean that you will wait for the elf to arrive tonight. I'm going to bed.

Edwin watched his mother go up the stairs to the bedroom. He didn't want to be alone, but he didn't want to go upstairs to go to bed either. So he watched the fire that, little by little, made smaller and smaller flames and was about to go out when the elf arrived.

"Hi, I'm Edwin. Who are you? Asked the child. "I am the elf. I come every night to order home when you are asleep." "I don't want to go to sleep! I'm not sleepy!" said Edwin. "I also don't want to sort and clean! Let's play," said the elf, and they jumped around the fire. Edwin wasn't tired; on the contrary, he wanted to jump and run more and more! The elf and the child jumped all night long enough to tire their legs. In the meantime, however, the fire had gone out and it was starting to get cold. "Edwin, I really have to start ordering now. It's my job," said the elf. "But I want to keep playing!" Edwin protested brightly. "Let's make a deal," said the elf. "Let's meet every night when the fire is about to go out and your mom is upstairs. We dance and play until the fire goes out and we say goodbye. If you go to sleep now, I'll come back tomorrow night to play with you" "Okay," Edwin agreed. "I'm going upstairs then, but don't tell mom anything." "Sssshhhh, she is coming, hide!" and the elf hid. Mom came down for a second to check on her baby. "Mom, I'm ready. Let's go to sleep now." "Well, I'm happy," Mom replied. "Let's go upstairs." Once in bed, Edwin fell asleep immediately, without making a fuss. The next evening, he asked his mother if he could be alone for a few minutes by the fire, and his mom accepted. The elf came and, together, they jumped and ran by the fire until they saw it go out. "Mom, I'm ready now," said the baby, and since then, he hasn't protested anymore to go to sleep.

Children's fairy tales about whims.

Dear mothers, this fairy tale is dedicated to whims. It is a story about emotions: it is part of those readings for children which, however, will also be good for adults. It is definitely recommended to understand how to behave with our little ones, but, above all, to understand what they feel and what we feel.

Sam the chameleon and the whims of the morning.

Sam is a chameleon who always throws a tantrum before going out. He starts saying no to everything and turns red. Whims are red, you know: it is the color of children who go on a rampage and cannot calm down. "I don't want to go out," he tells his mother on Monday morning before going to kindergarten. "I don't want to go out," he tells his mother on Saturdays before he goes shopping. "I don't want to go out," he says to his mother on Sundays when it's time to go to his grandparents for lunch.

When he throws a tantrum, Sam goes all red. Mother chameleon, in the beginning, is a set of perfectly mixed colors: a little orange, which means that she is always attentive and alert to what happens to her puppy; a little yellow, which indicates when she is happy. Suddenly a little blue arrives, enthusiasm:

"Sam, come on, a very large truck is passing by! We have to go out to see it better! Sam, however, is always red. "I don't want to go out and I don't like trucks!" "Okay," Mom says and turns all orange because she is thinking about how to persuade her chameleon and untie the knot of her whims.

"Shall we go out for breakfast this morning? From the bakery, I feel a good smell… " There is a speck of blue in her voice, but it is not understood very well. There is also a hint of red: it is small, but the chameleon cub sees it very well... Sam is too angry though. Red, fiery red. "I do not have breakfast. I don't want to go out." "Sam, it's very late now. At school, your friends are waiting for you; they have a new game in mind for this morning! "Mom tries to say, but the smile is no longer on her face and her voice is becoming serious. Mum is turning red too. "I DON'T WANT TO GO OUT!" Sam shouts. "Sam, it's time to go," Mom says and they are both really red. Mom is really annoyed at this point. She gets up, goes to the room to prepare the beds and whispers something in the ear of dad chameleon.

Chameleon's dad approaches Sam. "Let's play?" she says—Sam's eyes sparkle. "Let's have a race with the toy cars". Sam and dad get on the carpet to play. "Mine is faster," says Sam. "Eh, but you will see this..." "My carit has a steering wheel, lights and doors that can be opened! " Sam says happily. Now he is an all-blue chameleon! The minutes pass and the mother, fortunately, is still in the room tidying up. Dad whispers something in Sam's ear, "What are you saying, shall we go out now? Shall we surprise mum, can we put on shoes? "

When Mom comes back, Chameleon Dad and Sam are ready to go out! What color are they? All bright green, the color of calm.

"Dad is always green," Sam thinks and in the meantime, mum also calms down and, from her red that she was she, she gradually becomes orange, yellow and with a touch of green. "Mom, we can go out now," says Sam. He stopped throwing a tantrum.

Nora and the secret ingredient.

Once upon a time, there was a nice little girl named Nora. One fine afternoon Nora said to her mother, who in the meantime was busy with the housework: "Mom, I've finished all my homework! Can I go to my little room to play?" "Sure, darling," her mother replied.

But once in her room, the baby didn't start playing as she usually did. That day was a special day. Her father was having his birthday, and she wanted to give him a nice surprise. But what surprise? Think and think again, she finally got an idea, "I'll prepare a delicious cake with my toy kitchen!" she decided, all happy.

But which cake to prepare and how to prepare it? What was the father's favorite cake, "Mmm," she went back to mulling over the child to herself without knowing how to do it. While she was thinking, her mother came in carrying slices of bread and strawberry jam with a nice glass of milk: "It's snack time! I recommend you finish everything, so you become great! ".

Nora ate with great appetite and then, as she did every day, opened the window and left a few crumbs of her bread on the windowsill for the hungry birds. The mother went back to finish the chores and the child, continuing to think about which cake to prepare, went to her kitchen with her toy. She picked up a bowl and the wooden spoon, but as she did so, she heard a soft tapping coming out of the window. She looked up and saw that a sparrow had alighted on the windowsill and was pecking at the crumbs she had left behind. She looked at him well but without getting too close to not scare him. He was thin and cold; he looked so tired.

After getting sated, the little bird looked out with its head through the window that had remained ajar, opened its beak and exclaimed: "Thank you, thank you, little one, for saving me, I was really starving!" Nora stood petrified with her mouth wide open in amazement. She didn't believe her ears of hers, birds usually chirp, but they don't speak! "You don't have to be afraid of me," said the little bird seeing her frightened "In reality, I am not a sparrow, but a fairy who has been spelled. My name is Christel. And you?" "I'm Nora," said the child, widening her eyes and regaining her courage. "It's a very nice name," said the fairy. "Your room is also very nice! Can I come in?" Nora nodded yes, and Christel hopped into the room. He landed in the kitchen and exclaimed: "What a beautiful kitchen, it's a toy, but it lacks nothing! What good are you preparing?" "Today is my dad's birthday," replied the little girl, "and I wanted to surprise him by preparing him a special cake; I just don't know how to do it... I don't remember what his favorite cake is." "I can help you if you want," the fairy offered. "Siiiiii, thanks fairy!" Nora yelled happily.

"First we have to choose which cake to make" Christel said "When you cook for someone, you have to think not about what you like, but what he likes. What does your dad like best, then? " Mmm, thought Nora, he likes chocolate so much. "Very well, then it is decided: we will make a very soft and delicious chocolate cake" ruled the fairy "so as a second thing we have to prepare the ingredients that are: eggs, flour, sugar, cocoa powder, milk, oil and yeast and, in addition, The secret ingredient that makes everything we cook delicious. " Having said that, she gave a little wave with her wing and - poof! - all the ingredients appeared by magic.

"Wow!" Nora exclaimed in amazement, "It's all there, but ... can't I see the secret ingredient? I don't see it here, did you hide it ?. "Don't worry baby, we'll take her time," replied the fairy "Now, as a third thing, think about the gestures your mom makes when she prepares the cake and do the same too." "Yup!" the child said enthusiastically, then she peeled the eggs into the bowl and started to whisk them together with the sugar until she got a frothy mixture. She then added the oil, powdered chocolate and milk, always continuing to mix well. Finally, she also poured in the flour with the yeast. Once everything was well blended, she poured the mixture into the buttered pan.

"Very good Nora!" exclaimed the fairy. "Now, as a fourth thing, you need to know that every food put in the oven to cook needs the right temperature and the right cooking time. This cake should be placed in the preheated oven at 180 degrees for 30 - 35 minutes. And remember: as soon as you start to smell the cake, it means it's ready!"

The child turned on the oven, turned the knob to 180 degrees and when it was hot enough, again thanks to the fairy's magic touch, she put the cake pan in it. She closed it and after half an hour, the room was filled with a delicious fragrance. "It looks ready and judging by the scent; it must also be excellent!" Christel said smugly, looking through the oven glass. "Yes, we did it!" Nora exulted, taking out the cake. "It's almost dinner time and Dad will be back from work soon, just in time!".

"Very good! Only the last touch is missing, "said the fairy, recited a magic word, and the cake was covered with powdered sugar and colorful chocolate dragees.

"Thanks for helping me!" Nora exclaimed. "It was a pleasure; you are really a good girl," replied the fairy. "Now I have to fly away, but I'll come back to see you. And please, leave some crumbs of the cake on the windowsill for the birds." "Yes, I will. See you soon, fairy! " she greeted the child, but when Christel took off, she remembered Nora and shouted at her from the window, "Wait! Wait up!! We have forgotten the secret ingredient! " The fairy went back and always remaining in flight; she replied: "We have not forgotten, little one, the secret ingredient is Love. You put a lot of it into everything you do, that's why you are such a special and good girl! "And she walked away until she disappeared on the horizon.

Nora smiled, she was really happy, she had learned so many new things that afternoon and made a new friend. Later her father came home and the cake made with so much love was a huge surprise for him and for his mother. The little girl told them everything that had happened, leaving them greatly amazed, and in the end, they celebrated by eating many good things that her mother had also prepared. They made a toast for their father, for the whole family and for the new fairy friend Christel, so they all spent a cheerful and lively evening together, which remained in their memories forever.

Recipe for children: Soft Cake At Cocoa

If you want to make the cake, as it was described in the story, you need these ingredients:

300g of flour, 200g of milk, 180g of sugar, 100g of sugared cocoa (Nesquik or similar is fine too), 40 g of extra virgin olive oil (or 50 g of seed oil), 3 eggs, 1 sachet of baking powder, 1 26 cm butter cake pan

You can garnish the cake with powdered sugar, chocolate pralines, sugared almonds or fill it with cream, jam, whipped cream and fruit.

Soft cocoa cake - Nora is the secret ingredient

Preparation time

20 minutes

Cooking time

40 minutes

Total time

1 hour

If you want to make the cake, as it was described in the story, you need:

Ingredients
300 g of flour
300 g of flour
200 g of milk
200 g of milk
180 g of sugar
180 g of sugar
100 g of sweetened cocoa (Nesquik or similar is fine too)
100 g of sweetened cocoa (Nesquik or similar is fine too)
40 g of extra virgin olive oil (or 50 g of seed oil)
40 g of extra virgin olive oil (or 50 g of seed oil)

3 eggs

3 eggs

1 sachet of baking powder

1 sachet of baking powder

1 a 26 cm cake pan

1 a 26 cm cake pan

butter

Instructions

We use a food processor or electric whisk and need a donut mold

Beat the eggs with the sugar for a couple of minutes, add the Nesquik, then the oil and milk.

Always stirring, pour the vanilla and little by little flour 00 to which we have previously added the baking powder.

Grease and flour the mold, an operation that I do not do having used a silicone mold and pour our dough which will be a thick liquid and bake in a pre-heated static oven that we had brought to 180 ° temperature, this for a time between 35/40 minutes, but I always recommend doing the toothpick test in the last 5 minutes of cooking.

We take the mold out of the oven and let the donut with Nesquik cool completely to avoid breaking the cake.

Now we can decorate or cover as we like best and let's enjoy our dessert for a greedy moment of the day.

Note

You can garnish the cake with powdered sugar, chocolate pralines, sugared almonds, or fill it with cream, jam, whipped cream and melted chocolate.

www.ingramcontent.com/pod-product-compliance
Lightning Source LLC
Chambersburg PA
CBHW040106120526
44589CB00039B/2760